FUTURE
TRANSPORT
IN CITIES

Cities around the world are being wrecked by the ever-increasing burden of traffic. A significant part of the problem is the enduring popularity of the private car – still an attractive and convenient option to many, who turn a blind eye to the environmental and public health impact. Public transport has always seemed to take second place to the car, and yet alternative ways of moving around cities are possible. Measures to improve public transport, as well as initiatives to encourage walking and cycling, have been introduced in many large cities to decrease car use, or at least persuade people to use their cars in different ways.

This book explores many of the measures being taken, takes the best examples from around the world, and illustrates the work of architects and urban planners who have produced significant models of 'transport architecture' and city planning. It describes the ways in which new systems are evolving, and how these are being integrated into the urban environment. It suggests a future where it could be mandatory to provide systems of horizontal movement within large-scale development, using the technology of the lift, upon which every high-rise building depends. In so doing, future cities could evolve without dependence on the private car.

FUTURE
TRANSPORT
IN CITIES

BRIAN RICHARDS

SPON PRESS
Taylor & Francis Group

LONDON AND NEW YORK

First published 2001
by Spon Press
11 New Fetter Lane, London EC4P 4EE

Simultaneously published in the USA and Canada
by Spon Press
29 West 35th Street, New York, NY 10001

Spon Press is an imprint of the Taylor & Francis Group

Typeset in Helvetica Neue by Wearset Ltd, Boldon, Tyne and Wear
Printed and bound in Great Britain by St Edmundsbury Press,
Bury St Edmunds, Suffolk

British Library Cataloguing in Publication Data
A catalogue record for this book is available from the British Library

Library of Congress Cataloging in Publication Data
Richards, Brian, 1928–
    Future transport in cities/Brian Richards.
        p. cm.
    Includes bibliographical references and index.
        1. Local transit–Case studies.   2. City planning–Case studies.
        I. Title.

HE4211 .R468 2001
388.4–dc21   2001020830

ISBN 0-415-26142-2 (pbk)
ISBN 0-415-26141-4 (hbk)

for my grandchildren

Contents

Preface   In recent years, architects, industrial designers and others have been increasingly involved with the design of all aspects of public transport, from stations to bus stops and from interchanges to street design. It therefore seemed worthwhile to show how public transport is beginning to be integrated into the urban environment. To show the new systems that are being developed and how a future city might evolve, that provides mobility, yet reduces dependence on the private car.

The issue of what transport systems, apart from walking and cycling, are actually sustainable has not been defined. Most of the systems discussed rely on electricity, obtained from resources, some of which are renewable. In the future, buildings and layouts will increasingly be required to be sustainable. Finding a solution to the question of access to these buildings, to avoid them being surrounded by a sea of parked cars, is therefore an important part of the problem.

This book is not intended to be an attack on the private car. It aims instead to show that alternatives are possible. That cars could be used in different ways. That car dependence and individual ownership might be unnecessary. That in some cities, cars could become redundant. Cars have been allowed to wreak havoc on our cities and there are other ways of getting around, which can help to reduce the damage they have caused.

As to the future, with the arrival of the millennium, there is no sign that advances such as personal helicopters or airborne cars will result in a transport revolution, although it is perhaps too early to be sure of this. While not pursuing these developments, science fiction fans, it is hoped, will still find some of the more innovatory systems shown to be of interest.

Acknowledgements

Personal global transport (see Figure 8.38) from Baldwin J./1996 Bucky Works reprinted by permission of John Wiley & Sons Inc.

Among organisations who have supplied material: Adtranz, Alstom, Ballard, Bombardier, Bordeaux Metropole, Daimler-Chrysler, Honda Motor Co., Land Transport Authority and Urban Redevelopment Authority, Singapore, Nissan Motor Co., RATP Paris, Omron, Orestad Development Corporation, Copenhagen, Toyota Motor Corporation, Urbanisation of Curitiba Corporation (URBS), USTRA Hanover.

Among architects who have contributed: Ben van Berkel, Olivier Brochet, Richard Brosi, Ted Cullinan, Norman Foster, Frank Gehry, Zaha Hadid, Hackland & Dore, Ingenhoven, Overdiek and Partner, Arata Isozaki, Bernard Kohn and Pierre Vaysse, Rem Koolhaas, Richard Meier, Helmut Schulitz, Koichi Sone, Zimmer, Gunsul, Frasca, Partnership.

Special thanks to all those friends and contacts worldwide who beamed through much of the material. Leif Blomquist from Stockholm, Don Miles from Seattle, Ron Simpson from Vancouver, and many others too numerous to mention. Also to Polly Richards who read the script and offered many suggestions. Also my wife Sandra Lousada who took many of the pictures, and spent hours on the computer retrieving and improving material and riding on so many of the systems with me.

Photo-acknowledgements

Cover photo, Stan Smith/EMP.

Photos by the author: 1.2, 1.8, 1.9, 2.7, 2.14, 2.26, 3.1, 3.5, 4.6, 5.4, 5.5, 6.9, 6.32, 7.9, 7.20, 7.23, 8.49, 8.74, 8.80, 8.82, 8.84, 8.85, 8.88, 8.89. Helen Binet: 8.79. Stef Breukel: 7.19. Chorley & Hanford: 6.18, 7.4. Earwaker: 6.7. Strode Eckert: 2.11, 8.71. Eckert & Eckert: 2.9. Brice Forster: 2.13. Sandra Lousada: 2.27, 6.1, 6.2, 6.3, 6.5, 7.5, 7.7, 8.1, 8.67. National Film Archive/Transit Film GmbH 1. John Riach: 7.31, 7.43. Airdiasol Rothan: 8.77. Stan Smith/EMP: 6.10. Yoshio Tsukio: 7.30.

Every effort has been made to acknowledge correctly and contact the source and copyright holder of each picture and any errors or omissions will be corrected in future editions of the book.

Part I
The transport situation today

Chapter 1   Introduction

By the year 2000 many people believed that cities would be transformed. Streets would be quiet, safe places in which to walk and public transport would be a delight to use, being both convenient and affordable. In the cities of Western Europe, from which this book largely draws its material, some transport systems have, at least, partly achieved this. These cities are now better places in which to live and work, where people can bring up their kids safely and in good health. There has never been more of a demand by the public than today for a better environment in which to bring up their children. The 'image' for the city in which they live has become important for them – as has the ambition that, the city should be a 'delight' to be in, and a place to enjoy, rather than an environment torn apart by traffic.

In all cities an important factor affecting the environment is the numbers of cars per head of population (Europe, with a population density of 344 people per sq. mile, has 116 million cars while the United States (excluding Alaska) with a population density of 78 people per sq. mile has 141 million cars). How the car has been absorbed and dealt with by cities is discussed in this first section.

1.1 *facing page*
Set for the film *Metropolis*, directed by Fritz Lang in 1926. Possibly influenced by his first visit to New York, this portrayed life in a city where the workers lived and worked underground under protest, while their rulers enjoyed living above ground and travelled by various systems of transport.

The present situation

The predictions of car ownership in the UK are that a rise of 20 per cent could occur in the next ten years. Single-car ownership is increasing in the more affluent families to two or more cars. Although people love their cars, 50 per cent of the population still either do not own a car, cannot afford one, don't want one, or are

1.2
Grass roots opposition to more road building has questioned the need for more roads, which simply bring in more traffic. This protest, organised by residents of Hackney, an east London borough, concerned the East Cross route which was subsequently built.

too young – or too old – to drive. The effect on life in cities caused by traffic is already alarming. Three thousand children in the UK are killed or injured in an average year, which is the second highest accident rate in Europe, and vehicle exhaust is estimated to affect 200 million people in urban areas. According to the World Health Organisation 15,000 Italians die annually from smog-related illness. Noise levels too are estimated in Europe to affect over 80 million people. Pollution from traffic is also likely to have an effect on global warming, but the exact extent of this has yet to be established.

Some of the problems of traffic in cities are being dealt with by authorities with varying degrees of success. Depending on the country these may be summarised, somewhat simplistically, into five approaches towards the problem:

1. There is a serious and effective grass-roots opposition in most countries to more urban road-building on the basis that more roads mean more traffic.
2. Within residential areas there has been the development of traffic calming and town yards.
3. Controls on parking within city centres has effectively reduced and controlled the amount of traffic entering cities.
4. Planning laws are banning more out-of-town shopping centres or random car-oriented development.
5. Public transport has been maintained and improved, without which none of the other measures would be effective.

In spite of these measures there remains the nagging problem associated with continuing car growth, the political strength of the car lobby and a public wanting to use cars. People love their cars. Cars are a retreat from the real world, which partly accounts for their popularity. Cars also afford a degree of comfort and privacy for the user which public transport does not, and can take the driver where he or she wants to go. As a result of this, the car has caused the most problems to city life. It is here that alternative ways must be found of providing transport which is good enough to get people out of their cars, as well as providing a better service for those without them.

Cars in cities: what is happening

In the 1960s a project by an American architect, Victor Gruen for Fort Worth, Texas, represented a prototypical image for the planners of many European cities after the Second World War. Gruen's plan showed a city centre with a pedestrian-only centre about 1 km square, with small bus-trains serving as local transport.

The deck was to be serviced from basement level and ringed by a giant freeway system, feeding into multi-storeyed parking for 60,000 cars. Many German cities were rebuilt along similar lines, except that the ring roads were smaller and public transport by bus or rail still served the centres. Most of the city centres adopted pedestrian-only areas for their main shopping streets but built multi-storeyed car parks around them because at that time it was believed essential to their survival.

These parking buildings, together with the inner ring roads built later, proved not only to be inadequate for the numbers of cars entering and wanting to park, but frequently occupied valuable land as well as generating unwanted traffic. In Essen, for example, the ring road serving the parking has had to be expensively bridged in order to connect the centre with the surrounding neighbourhoods. Such roads became nooses around the centres, overscaled and isolating them from the surrounding neighbourhoods. Work on Munich's only partly built inner ring road was, in fact, abandoned once the populace realised what it was going to do to the city centre.

Park and ride

In European cities it was found that some people still wanted to live close to the centres, if not in them. As car ownership increased so parking became insufficient and much of it, principally commuter parking, was moved to the periphery, accessible from outer ring roads, smaller than in Gruen's plan. More importantly it became obvious to site this parking next to rail or light rail routes which people could use to reach the centres more quickly than driving. Hamburg, for example, froze parking in the centre and constructed, at least one well-planned park and ride garage adjoining its subway line, providing ticket machines at every level with lifts feeding directly down to platform level. But this attention to detail is rare. All too often, for reasons of cost, where land was cheap, park and ride was built at surface level around the suburban stations, creating a barrier for anyone walking to the station. San Francisco's BART metro planned many of its suburban stations in this way, regardless of the environmental implications, but is now rectifying this by beginning to build multi-storeyed parking, as well as offices, on sites of former car parks. Moreover, due to the presence of the station, the land values have risen.

Light rail today is increasingly used to serve park and ride commuters and shoppers although operators are rarely obliged to pay the high price of multi-storeyed parking (see Figure 2.10). Because light rail is so often retrofitted into an existing community (such as has occurred in Vancouver with its Skytrain, or in Croydon with London's Tramlink), park and ride car parks are deliberately omitted at stations in order to reduce the traffic generated by them. Instead passengers reach stations on foot, by cycle or by bus – or are simply dropped or picked up at stations ('kiss and ride').

Not all countries have followed this practice. France, for example, which has had a long-standing honeymoon with the car, continues to build extensive multi-level parking around its stations. Some 100,000 car spaces are provided on the periphery of Paris, often without parking controls in neighbouring communities. For example at Torcy, served by the Regional Express metro line (RER), the multi-level parking for 1000 cars is unused and commuters simply park free in the surrounding streets. Within the city centres, any new building in France will normally be required to provide for layers of parking below, and architects take this as a matter of course, giving their buildings, in cross section, the appearance of an iceberg (see Figure 7.3). It was not for nothing that President Pompidou decreed 'it is necessary to adapt Paris for the automobile' and did so, destroying both banks of the Seine with motorways in the process.

This approach contrasts with policies for new office building in the City of London where developers are not required to provide for parking unless their clients feel it is necessary to pay the high cost of doing this. What should also be done is to require, as occurs in France, that anyone working in the centre employing more than ten people contribute towards the cost of the transport infrastructure by enacting a tax (*le versement public*) based on a percentage of the wages paid. This tax raises substantial sums of money in France to help finance new transport infrastructure. For example in Strasbourg £34 million is raised annually for subsidising public transport and £61 million was raised by this means to help finance the construction of the light rail system, which cost £230 million (Hass-Klau *et al.*, 2000).

The insatiable demand for parking space, and the traffic congestion caused by cars looking for parking space, has now resulted in planning authorities, in parts of North America, enacting controls to limit the amount of car access to new developments, before planning permission is granted. Employers in some areas of California, for example, are required to reduce parking by encouraging their employees to reach their workplace by sharing cars (called car-pooling) or alternatively by providing them with small self-driven buses to serve groups of fellow workers living in the same area (called van-pooling). Workers too, may be given free travel passes for use on trains or buses. At Boots, in Nottingham UK, for example, over £250,000 a year is spent on providing special buses to bring workers to its factory (Transport 2000).

1.3
Van poolers at 3M factory, Minneapolis. A popular means of transport for suburban commuters in North America, with vans often paid for by the factory and driven by the workers, with priority space given for parking. Courtesy: 3M, Minnesota.

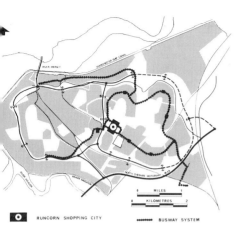

RUNCORN SHOPPING CITY   BUSWAY SYSTEM

1.4
Runcorn, UK. A new town of 70,000 people
built in the 1960s around a 12 mile figure-of-
eight bus-only road. Stops are all five minutes'
walk from homes built at a density of 173
persons/ha. The busway remains well-used by
the two bus companies, now being upgraded
to provide disabled access to the stops.

1.5
View of busway, then segregated, to run below
pedestrian routes. The stops are now being
amended with grade level crossings for
disabled access, eliminating steps, bridges or
subways. Courtesy: Halton Borough Council.

Moving around residential areas

Low-density residential areas with as few as 30 houses to the acre are commonplace in the UK. This is around half the density of those built on the Continent and,
combined with high car ownership, such densities are too low to make public
transport economic to run (see Chapter 7). London suburbs that grew up specula-
tively along the new tubelines were originally within walking distance of the stations, built with shops around them. In recent years, however, suburban
development has occurred on greenfield sites with little regard for how public
transport could serve it and car-oriented shopping centres have been built remote
from stations. As a result the original shops, clustered around suburban tube stations, have been allowed to decay. Bus services too are rarely able to give a good
enough service to tempt people onto them, once they have purchased cars, or
worse still, their second car if they can afford it.

One notable example of transport integration into a residential area was made
in the UK at Runcorn, near Liverpool, with a population of 70,000 people. Built in
the 1960s with housing at densities of 173 persons/hectare (70 persons/acre),
Runcorn was laid out around a figure-of-eight segregated busway which ran
through its town centre, with stops along it a maximum of five minutes' walk from
homes. Today this is now something of a landmark and the whole layout is being
refurbished to make access for the disabled (see Figure 1.5).

Milton Keynes with a population now of around 200,000 people, was laid out
on a road grid of 1–2 km squares, within which each neighbourhood of 5,000
people was served originally by Dial-a-Ride. This used small radio-controlled
buses whose route was selected by computer – not unlike today's computer-
taxis. These picked up people who phoned for a ride and took them to their
required destination. The system was disbanded, however, because half the
population did not have phones and because it was expensive to run. Many of
the housing layouts consisted of cul-de-sacs, dead-end roads, and much of the
housing was approached by pathways so that the buses could not arrive at
the front doors or circulate easily from one area to another. Today at Milton
Keynes public transport is poor, and car ownership high. Conventional buses now
follow the grid roads, giving a service a long way from what was originally intended
with shared taxis a popular means of transport for many, particularly from the principal shopping centre.

As housing densities increase, so parking space takes up more land at ground
level, which should be used for parks and play spaces. Parking consequently has
to be put underground which is expensive, or in multi-storeyed structures. This
allows for the remainder of a development to be denser, with shorter walking distance and no wasteland for ground level parking in between.

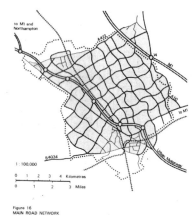

Figure 16
MAIN ROAD NETWORK

1.6

Milton Keynes, UK. A heavily car-oriented city for 200,000 people with a grid of roads of from 1 to 2 km, enclosing each 5,000 person neighbourhood.

1.7

Typical street pattern within a neighbourhood at Milton Keynes. The housing was intended to be served by radio-controlled dial-a-ride buses to be called for by phone to pick up people at their doors. The cul-de-sac layouts were difficult to run services on economically, and dial-a-ride has now been replaced by conventional buses running on the main road grid. Courtesy: Milton Keynes Development Corporation.

In many countries in Europe cycling within residential areas has become popular (European Commission). This has occurred where special provision for safe cycling has been built and segregated cycleways have been provided alongside existing main roads in the town and city centres, notably in Holland and Denmark. Today well-planned housing development should provide for cycleways from the outset, although totally segregating this from the road layout is not always successful. At Milton Keynes, the largest cycleway network in the UK – the 200 km long Redway – has not proved to be a success, partly for reasons of design, maintenance and the difficulty of providing personal security (Franklin, 1999). This is partly because the routes run largely through green spaces and not beside the main road system. However cities like Copenhagen have successfully encouraged mass cycling, with 300 km of cycle lanes, provided by its main roads within the centre. The result is that 30 per cent of the working population now use cycles to get to work.

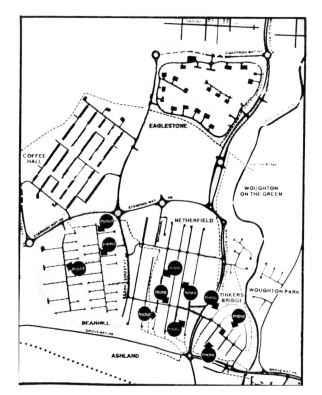

1.9 *above*
Cycling in Hiroshima. One of the best used methods of transport to reach metro stations in the country.

1.8 *above*
Separate cycle lanes in Utrecht, Holland. One lane at each side of the main roads in the centre is given over for cycling, normal practice in a country with a tradition for safe cycling.

1.10
Copenhagen, Denmark. Map showing 300 km (186 miles) of cycle paths provided beside all existing regional roads and distributor streets, used by 30 per cent of commuters daily. New cycle routes are being built, aimed at increasing the length of average cycling trips from 5 to 15 km. Courtesy: Copenhagen Municipality, Lord Mayor's Dept.

Chapter 2   Improving public transport

Providing for convenient, safe, regular and reliable public transport is an essential requirement for any urban area and basically three types of public transport are used in cities, either separately or in conjunction with one another. They are buses and trolley buses, light rail (trams) and railways. Each system is chosen as best suited for the job it has to do, depending on the number of people to be carried or the distance to be travelled. Public transport routes and the systems used have evolved in existing cities over many years. They may be out of date, overloaded or no longer economic to run and require replacing with new systems better suited for the job. This applies particularly to bus systems which have for too long been regarded as a second-rate form of transport.

In expanding cities new areas of development must be planned around public transport, either by using buses, as has been done in Curitiba, Brazil, or other systems such as light rail as in Portland, Oregon. When this is done the systems can be integrated into development unimpeded by problems of the existing infrastructure such as occurs in existing cities.

Buses

Buses are the workhorse of any city transport network and for years have been unfairly considered a second-rate system of transport because they used out-of-date vehicles operating on congested streets with other traffic. In recent years new bus design, cleaner engines and the infrastructure now being provided in the way of bus-only lanes have helped improve their image. The range of buses now

2.1
Overhead view of the Curitiba busway, where the central reservation is used by double-articulated express buses. Courtesy: URBS.

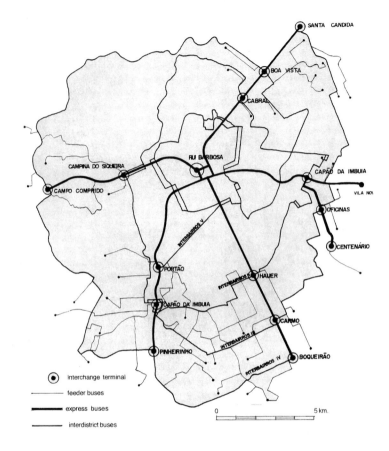

2.2

Curitiba, Brazil. A city with a population of 1.6 million, laid out around five boulevards radiating from the centre. Each of the boulevards has two-way express bus lanes in the centre. Interchange stops, shown circled, are served by local feeder buses. Courtesy: URBS.

available is wide and vehicle size will depend on the loading requirement. For example, on the heavily used radial corridors of Curitiba, Brazil, special double-articulated Volvo express buses carrying 200 people run on bus-only lanes in the centre of the boulevards fanning out radially from the city centre. These carry up to 15,000 people an hour – a figure comparable to the capacity of a light rail system. In less dense neighbourhood areas small buses act as feeder buses to the main ones carrying only 15–20 people and interchanging with the express buses at specially designed stops (see Figures 2.3, 2.4).

Buses are now built with low floors for easy access, particularly important for disabled passengers. Wide doors reduce the time spent at stops for boarding or leaving. Buses are now equipped with on-board location systems operated via satellite which automatically show the driver if he is running on time. Bus stops will have 'real-time' information boards showing passengers when the next bus will come. London will have 6,500 bus stops equipped with these on 700 routes in the next two years. Vehicles can also be fitted with transponders which turn traffic lights in their favour at junctions. Developments with guided buses (see p. 103) allow them to use narrower roads as well as guiding them accurately alongside raised bus stops which permit safe wheelchair boarding at the same level.

Bus stops are normally placed at 300–400 metre intervals throughout urban areas and are usually minimal structures affording poor weather protection. This minimal design of stops possibly accounts for the decreasing number of people using buses, particularly in winter conditions, where they afford poor protection. In Curitiba, Brazil, bus stops provide good weather protection, as well as providing for ticketing. Here circular glass tubes are raised to line up with bus floor level and are entered or exited from either end, via steps or a lift to allow for wheelchair access. This cuts boarding time by an estimated one-quarter compared to conventional stops. However, their size restricts their use to wide pavements.

2.3
Curitiba's tubular bus stops have floors raised to the same level as the bus floors. Drivers follow a painted line on the road to steer close to the stops. Courtesy: URBS.

2.4
Detail of Curitiba bus stop showing the platform extended from the bus to bridge the gap and permit wheelchair boarding. Steps and a lift are situated at the end of the stops to give access to turnstiles. Courtesy: URBS.

Experiments are being tried out in Hong Kong with pre-bought ticketing machines, swipe cards or smart cards which deduct the fare as one enters and can be charged up at special machines or banks when they run out of units. These help reduce boarding time at stops but there have been virtually no developments with any radical bus stop designs which give passengers serious weather protection and which can be integrated into existing streets. New bus terminals, possibly because they are supervised, are often fully enclosed, heated or air-conditioned, with shops, cafes and seats where passengers wait in the warm and dry behind automatic glass doors which open for boarding, when the bus arrives. A system called 'pulse-scheduling' is also being tried, where buses are timed to arrive at an interchange point the same time as other buses are about to leave going in other directions. This minimises waiting times for passengers changing – an example of 'seamless interchange'. In terms of value for money, buses as a form of transport cannot be disputed. However, this does not necessarily mean that a bus system will attract enough people on to it to make it profitable. A new air-conditioned articulated bus carrying 125 passengers costs around one-tenth of that of a new light rail vehicle carrying 200 passengers, although it may only have a ten-year life compared to a thirty-year life for light rail. However running costs per passenger are frequently shown to be more expensive on buses than light rail. Buses provide an essential part of any city transport system, either running on their own in smaller cities or working as feeder systems.

Guided buses have proved to be successful in Adelaide, South Australia (see p. 135). Here they circulate within residential areas on ordinary roads before entering a guideway where they continue to the city centre. France is experimenting with a number of alternative guidance systems (see p. 137) and will use overhead power lines to provide electric power, like a trolley bus. However whether bus route corridors create new areas of development or growth is debatable. In

2.5
Curitiba, Brazil. Cross section showing high-rise offices and luxury residential apartments facing the main boulevards, with express buses running in the centre. Smaller buses serve the lower density areas on either side. Source: Instituto de Peisquisa e Plannejamento Urbano de Curitiba. IPPUC.

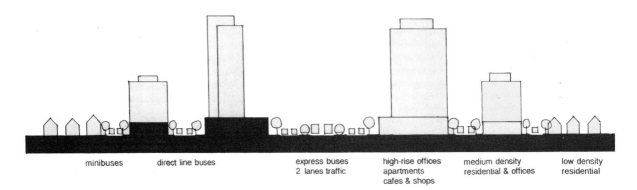

minibuses   direct line buses   express buses   high-rise offices   medium density   low density
                                               2 lanes traffic   apartments   residential & offices   residential
                                                                       cafes & shops

Curitiba high-rise luxury development has occurred along the principal boulevards carrying the express bus routes, yet paradoxically these are where homes for the wealthy with high car ownership exist. In Ottawa at stations along the bus-only, segregated Transitway (see p.133) some development has occurred (Cervero, 1998) but these are exceptional cases.

Politicians and developers rightly regard light rail as something tangible which has a degree of permanence and which, once built, will not disappear, as can happen to a bus route. Light rail, as has been shown at Portland, can encourage new development to occur along it, and help improve the 'image of the city'. In Strasbourg, for example, property values along the light rail routes are 10 per cent higher than elsewhere. Today it is the construction of light rail routes, not bus routes, that are recognised by planners as a way of restructuring a city, at far less cost than building a conventional metro. In Europe today, light rail is being given priority lanes to run on and takes up road space that was previously full of traffic. As a result its construction is seen as a way of actually reducing traffic within the city, yet is still regarded as acceptable politically.

Light rail: an alternative to trams

Light rail has become one of the success stories of public transport in recent years, now running in over 100 cities worldwide. Traditional trams, in the past, were often removed 'because they got in the way of traffic'. Today, with much-improved vehicles, any well-planned system gives trams priority over other traffic. The vehicles are articulated, capable of high acceleration and of running at average speeds of 17–20 kph (10–12 mph) with top speeds of 30–40 kph (18–25 mph). They carry from 200 to 280 passengers depending on their length (33–43 m long) with low floors for easy boarding and they cost over £1 million each.

The popularity of light rail with the public has helped increase overall use of public transport where they have been built with buses frequently acting as feeder systems to stations. They also attract people out of driving, possibly because of their greater reliability, speed and comfort. An average 11 per cent of new passengers who previously drove have been found to use light rail in 14 European cities. In Strasbourg 17,000 bus passengers on one route increased to 65,000 four years later when it was upgraded to light rail (Hass-Klau). Light rail today is being skilfully integrated into the fabric of cities, although the cost of this can add over 60 per cent to that of a basic system (see pp.142–151). In Zurich in 1988 it was decided that instead of building a subway costing £375 million an upgraded bus and tram system would cost only £100 million. This now gives priority over other

2.6 *overleaf*
Strasbourg, France. A city of 430,000 people, showing the low-floor trams in the city centre, by the industrial designer Philippe Neerman. The Eurotram shown is low-floor, air-conditioned, carrying up to 270 passengers. The stops are each 45 m long, 240 mm high, to allow for level boarding. Courtesy: Adtranz.

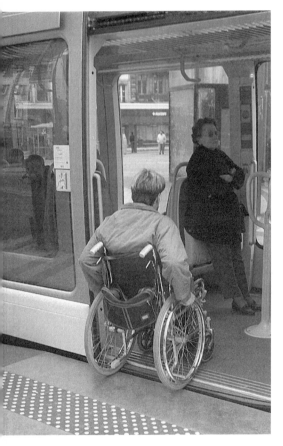

2.7
Raised platforms serving low-floored trams and guided buses allow direct access for wheelchair users, improving boarding times by up to 35 per cent.

traffic at 270 light-controlled junctions and its citizens have the best used bus and rail system in Europe. An average 800 trips per person are made by public transport in a year in Zurich, the highest in Europe, compared to London's 270 trips or Manchester's 75 trips (Hass-Klau et al., 2000).

Light rail in city centres   Light rail running at ground level may, as occurs in Grenoble, France, run down the centre of a pedestrianised street. In other cases it may take over only part of a wide roadway and be placed at one side. Stops are normally at 400 m intervals, although in Zurich they are closer at 370 m intervals. They are now generally low, 350 mm high to provide for boarding for the disabled and others at the same level as the vehicle floor. Within pedestrian areas the elimination of all vehicular traffic, except for servicing at certain hours, is now more readily accepted by shopkeepers, previously opposed to car-free areas with the insertion of light rail. This gives vitality to the streets, provides excellent access for large numbers of people and being non-polluting is regarded more favourably than buses. In certain situations, for example, in order to cross below railway lines, as in Rouen or Strasbourg, light rail may run partially underground which is around seven times more expensive than at surface level. A section of the light rail system being planned for Dublin, running north from St Stephen's Green, for example, will run underground because the road system is too narrow to find a right of way for a two-way system. However when stops are built underground they have to be served by escalators and lifts to make them easily accessible.

Suburban travel   Within residential areas light rail, as in the city centre, requires its own right of way over traffic and the intervals between stops will vary according to the densities or the distance to be travelled. In Zurich, for example, stops at 370 m intervals are closer together than bus stops (Hass-Klau et al., 2000). Wider spacing of stops can mean that the distances to them are too far to walk. Beyond a 500 m radius to homes, cycle parking has to be provided, as well as feeder buses with drop-down areas at each station both for the buses and for kiss and ride. Portland, Oregon is an example where light rail is intended to restructure the communities through which it passes. Here a new 29 km (18 mile) long line, the Westside Max, runs through existing low-density suburban areas and acquisition of 1500 acres of land around the stations is allowing for denser development to occur with small shops, apartments and offices all within walking distance of the stops.

Like a metro line, light rail, used to serve park-and-ride commuters, can present the problem of stations being surrounded by a parking wasteland, disliked by those living nearby and has to be crossed by people walking to stations. Strasbourg has taken 1000 parking spaces out of the city centre (see p. 145) with

2.8
Portland, Oregon's downtown showing the two transit malls on which run the light rail system. Since installation employment in the centre has risen from 50,000 to 100,000 people with no increase in parking and 90 per cent of people riding there by bus or light rail are car owners. Courtesy: Tri-Met.

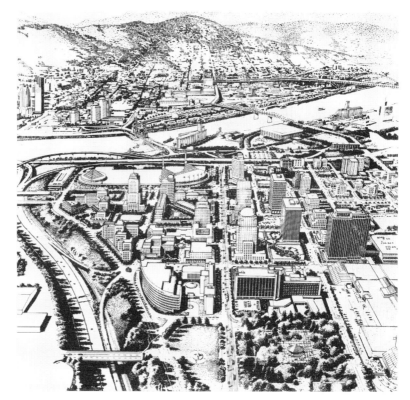

2.9
Night-time view showing lift towers and entrance plaza illumination. Architects: Zimmer, Gunsul, Frasca, Partnership.

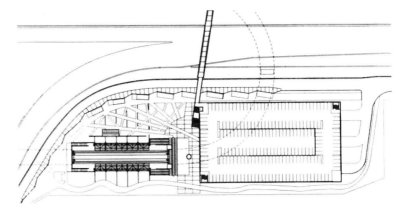

2.10
Transit Centre block plan showing multi-level, free, parking garage for 630 cars adjoining the station, planned to eliminate surface parking around it.

2.11

Typical light rail stop on the transit mall in the centre of Portland where 90 per cent of riders are car owners. Courtesy: Tri-Met.

2.12
Portland's Sunset Transit Centre set in cutting with lift enclosures in glass blocks, brilliantly lit up at night. Architects: Zimmer, Gunsul, Frasca, Partnership.

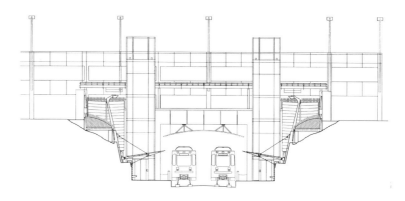

2.13
Cross section through Transit Centre showing overhead glazed platform canopies integrated into the column supports, combined with lighting.

paying parking provided at the end of the light rail lines and the cost of the parking ticket giving free use of the light rail. Some stations in Portland provide for multi-storeyed parking (see Figure 2.10) for 500–600 cars adjacent to the main road system, but for reasons of cost this is rarely done. In Vancouver, the second stage of the 21 km (13 mile) long elevated and driverless Skytrain, built over main roads (see Figure 6.12), through existing communities, has 13 stations providing drop-down space only, for kiss-and-ride use, for bus access and cycle parking. The stations instead aim to become a focal point in the community with a news stand, small shops or snack bar, to help create pedestrian activity. These provisions and the alignment of the elevated system were the result of having community discussions with more than 100,000 people.

The rebirth of the railways

Railways, long in a decline in many cities, are now being reborn, attracting passengers as traffic congestion on the roads has become worse. Added to this is the high cost of shortage of parking within city centres. Short-haul inter-city air travel has frequently become so congested and airports so overcrowded that on many routes high-speed inter-city expresses, for distances of 650 km (400 miles) and over, are proving to be quicker and so are taking away their passengers.

Basically three kinds of railways serve cities:

1. long-distance railways which include high-speed inter-city expresses;
2. regional metros which serve the region around the city; and
3. local and suburban railways, which run to the boundary of the city and include metros.

High-speed rail travel   High-speed inter-city expresses started with the Tokaido Express in Japan which effectively linked the main cities on the east coast. This was followed by the TGV (Train à Grande Vitesse) in France, which now links with high speed lines to cover the countries of Western Europe. The Eurostar, running through the Channel Tunnel between London, Paris and Brussels, links to this at Lille (see Figure 2.15) and has successfully captured 63 per cent of the air traffic between those cities. The most recent major achievement is the bridge linking Mälmo, Sweden, with Copenhagen. The success of these high-speed services, running between city centres, has led to heavy investment in new stations, notably in France, and the upgrading of existing ones to a high standard. The work being done by the Station Design Office of the French National Railways with AREP, a multi-disciplinary team of architects and engineers, aims to give the public a new concept of rail travel, through good design. Cities like Lille, and most recently Marseille, have welcomed the arrival of high-speed services because it helps to project a forward-thinking image and it is believed that its arrival will help attract businesses to locate there.

In Lille, for example, in the north of France, the original TGV route was planned to by-pass the city, but through political pressure from the mayor was diverted and now has a new station called Eurolille, planned by architect Rem Koolhaas. In addition to offices located above the station concourse, adjacent to it is a new conference centre and shopping centre which helps tie the station with the old centre. The infrastructure built to support this development, with new roads, parking and good suburban rail links, has been successful in transforming an indifferent area into a substantial business centre with the centres of Paris and London just over an hour away in either direction. Similarly, operators of conventional railways are upgrading their stations and combining them with new development. Developers who were 10 years ago insistent that their projects were solely accessible by cars are now demanding that they should be served by rail stations as well, often paying for the construction costs.

The growth of fast inter-city rail transport makes good 'seamless' interchange with other modes of transport all the more important. Passengers arriving are 'captive' to whatever transport is available – metro, bus or tram or taxi. Transferring easily and quickly on to these systems is essential and many cities and towns have built fine interchange stations to deal with this. Chur, Switzerland, although

2.14 *left*

Lille, France. Eurostar interchange station serving trains bound for London, Paris and Brussels. View of concourse showing TGV (Train à Grande Vitesse) with the lines on left serving the south of France, running parallel with Eurostar lines. The roof is designed by Peter Rice.

2.15 *below*

Lille Eurostar station. Plan by Rem Koolhaas and OMA showing the main concourse at the top (2) adjoining the Val, automatic underground metro (3). The motorway feeds directly into the underground parking running parallel to the tracks. Three office buildings straddle the concourse. A shopping centre by Jean Nouvel, adjoins the station and links with the old rail terminus (1) serving the regional train services. The main square of Lille is situated beyond this and has been pedestrianised. Courtesy: Office for Metropolitan Architecture.

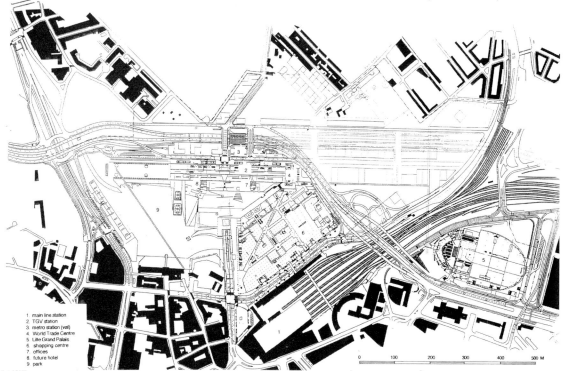

1. main line station
2. TGV station
3. metro station (val)
4. World Trade Centre
5. Lille Grand Palais
6. shopping centre
7. offices
8. future hotel
9. park

0   100   200   300   400   500 M

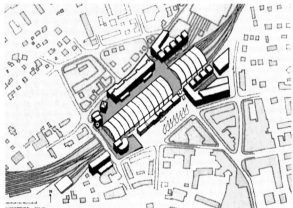

2.16 *top*
Chur, Switzerland. A major transport interchange serving a station and the ski resorts of St Moritz and Davos. Serving 6,000 skiers a day in winter who interchange from trains to the buses. View of glazed roof covering bus station above rail tracks, designed by Peter Rice.

2.17 *left*
Block plan. Buildings on either side of the tracks are offices and post office.

2.18 *bottom*
Long section showing bus deck covered by a glazed roof, with escalator and lift access to the rail platforms below.

2.19 *facing page*
Escalators serving bus station above rail platforms. Architects: Richard Brosi and Robert Obrist.

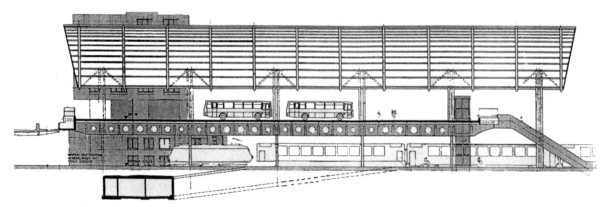

essentially serving tourist traffic is still a classic example of an interchange station (see pp. 22, 23). This station handles around 6,000 skiers a day in winter who arrive by train and leave by the 200 buses which circulate above the tracks with interchange protected from the weather under a fine roof.

The problems, however, in those cities, often with historic nineteenth-century terminal rail stations, located at the edge of the central area, are how to best serve the new high-speed lines. Lille has been discussed, where the station serves the express tracks. These bypass the old terminal station which is still in use, serving the regional trains. Florence is planning a similar station, for through services, adjacent to its present terminal. Stuttgart (see p. 25), following an architectural competition, is planning a new through station for express lines below Castle Gardens, an historic park in the centre with 'glass eyes' appearing above, lighting the platforms below. In contrast to this well considered scheme, Paris built its Regional Express (RER) interchange, serving all four lines on the site of the old market, Les Halles, demolishing the historic market buildings and replacing them with an inferior formal park and shopping centre. London, where originally through Eurostar services would have passed under the centre through an underground station at King's Cross, has since then planned to terminate these trains at St Pancras, one of its finest stations. This will be almost doubled in length to accommodate the Eurostar trains.

The importance of providing for good access to airports by rail as well as by road is now seen to be essential with airports connected not only to city centres but also to the regional rail network. Schiphol, Holland, for example, has built a well-designed new station as part of the airport, with a glazed concourse, giving direct access to trains below, running to Amsterdam and the Dutch towns, as well as providing express services to Berlin, Brussels or Paris. London's Paddington now has baggage facilities for airport passengers. Baggage, after being checked in by the passenger, is put on to conveyor belts, running below the platforms and manually handled on to express trains reaching Heathrow in 15 minutes, which would take over an hour by road.

New stations, and those being updated, are an essential element in any future city and potential growth points for new development such as for offices combined with shopping. As a result much is being made by developers and railway authorities who see this as a means of paying for a new station. While there may be space over some stations and around them for this to occur, many are already in congested areas. Rather than simply add to the congestion in the area the first priority should lie in providing better access and egress for the ever-increasing numbers of passengers using the trains.

Metro and rapid transit systems
Extensive metro systems in the large cities such as Paris, New York, Tokyo or London were built when labour was cheap. Many of them, now nearly 100 years old, have been continually extended and

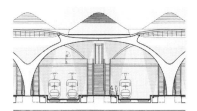

2.21
Model of typical roof light and structural support above platforms.

2.20
Stuttgart, Germany. Winning design for a new through station to serve high-speed trains, to be situated below a public park in the city centre. Cross section through station platforms showing roof lights integrated with supporting roof structure. Illustration by Peter Wels.

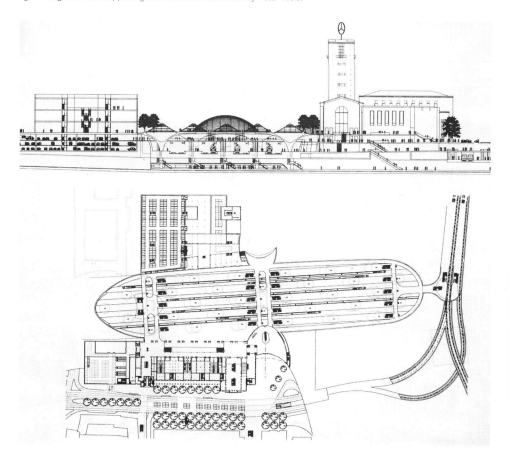

2.22
Long section and platform level plan showing upper concourse within historic building, linked to platforms by stair, lifts and escalators. Architects: Ingehoven, Overdiek and Partner.

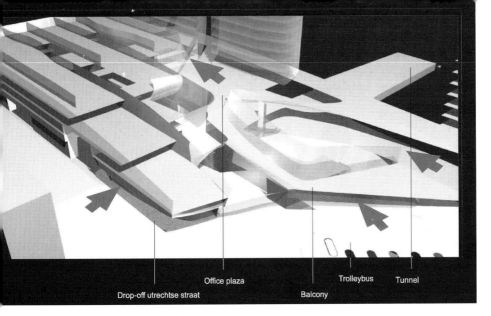

Office plaza

Trolleybus

Tunnel

Drop-off utrechtse straat

Balcony

2.23

Arnhem, Holland. Transport interchange. An integrated transport project using digital information on pedestrian and vehicular movement to generate a dynamic form to the buildings. High-level view of model showing trolley bus terminal on right, with the pedestrian tunnel on the left leading to the station platforms on the right.

2.24

Model of part of station looking along trolley bus islands with offices in the distance. Architects: van Berkel with Ove Arup.

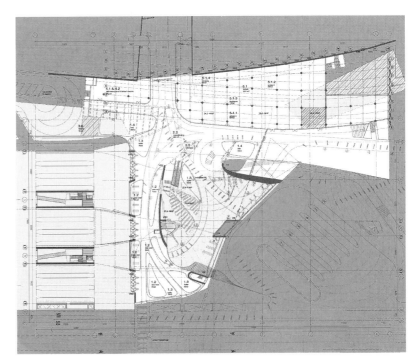

2.25

Plan of central node of station, with entrance passage to station platform at top, bus station on the left with trolley bus terminus on the right. A ramped slab leads down to cycle and car parking below.

upgraded over the years. New systems, in spite of their high cost, are still being built, such as in Mexico City, Shanghai, or Hong Kong and are heavily used. But because of the high cost of going underground there is growing interest in building elevated systems, monorails, or even heavy rail systems above ground, provided that the environmental problems associated with them can be overcome (see p. 56).

The new regulations governing the planning of underground stations have added considerably to their cost. Factors such as planning for means of escape, how to evacuate platforms in four minutes and providing ventilation systems which can quickly get rid of smoke rapidly are now seen to be essential. These requirements can have considerable impact, visually at surface level. With overhead systems many of these problems are resolved but the visual impact on a city centre of tracks and stations is considerable. The development of land immediately adjacent to stations either above or below ground is also important.

In Arnhem, Holland, for example, the existing station is being redeveloped to an imaginative plan by architect Van Berkel (see Figure 2.23, 2.24). Here a new shop-lined pedestrian link with the town centre will connect with a bus and trolley-bus terminus, situated beside the station. Below this will be parking for cars and cycles with new offices above.

Many of the Dutch stations designed by Holland Railconsult, such as Leiden (Edwards, 1997), have been rebuilt to better serve the community. This is often a problem where lines sever sections of a town centre. Leiden, for example, handling 40,000 passengers a day, now has a shop-lined, largely daylit, and generous pedestrian underpass running below the 12 tracks above, leading from a newly planned town square, served by a bus terminus which connects both sides of the town together.

Station design

The planning and design of stations is complex and architects are now involved, working alongside engineers from the conceptual stage. With the need to project a good image to the public, rail operators now recognise the importance of imaginative station design. This is particularly important in underground station design, previously done by engineers, partly because people prefer to travel above ground rather than underground. Factors such as providing daylight down to platform level are now seen to be important. The new underground stations on the metro at Bilbao (see p. 54) by Foster architects, and stations on the Paris Meteor line by Kohn and Vaysse, have brought a new dimension to underground travel. Similarly on London's Jubilee extension the success of bringing light down to the platform levels of several of the stations has helped add some 'delight' to underground travel.

As cities grow, with road traffic at saturation levels, travel on all systems of public transport will increase and if cities are to survive this will require increasingly heavy investment and, above all, good planning and design.

2.26
Leiden, Holland. View of unticketed concourse running below tracks, linking both sides of the town together, lined with attractive shops, two cafes and open all day.

2.27

Paris, France. View of Chatelet station on the new Meteor line showing hoops crossing over the tracks supporting continuous glazed automatic doors along the platform edges. The driverless trains designed by Roger Tallon run at two-minute intervals. Architects: Kohn & Vaysse.

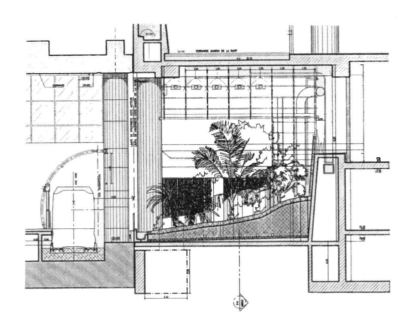

2.28

Paris, Meteor Gare de Lyon station showing tropical garden beside the line. Tropical plants are automatically sprinkled and thrive in the temperature of the metro. The garden also brings light to the platforms. Landscape architects: Gunig and Tribel. Architects: Kohn & Vaysse.

Chapter 3

Towards a better environment

Pressures, in larger existing cities, to avoid developing in the historic core have led to alternative strategies of growth being adopted and to the planning of sub-centres, like La Défense in Paris or London Docklands Canary Wharf (Chapter 7). Both these differ from the so-called 'edge cities' in the United States which are almost totally car-dependent for access. Instead they have been built to a greater density with housing as part of them or adjacent and with access provided by good public transport. Parking for private cars, though, is in excess of the road systems serving them, with La Défense having parking for 20,000 cars and 10,000 cars at Canary Wharf.

There will always be pressure from landowners and politicians to keep historic centres alive and those with quality are likely to remain popular with the public as well as with tourists. In the City of London, its business centre, for example, many foreign banks still prefer to build their headquarters there, rather than go to London's Canary Wharf. This is due partly to tradition, as well as the fact that it is closer to where its executives want to live.

Bringing back walking

In historic city centres the quality of the walking environment is important, and something to be enjoyed, and today most of Europe's city centres are now traffic free, or at least have given over large areas of road space for pedestrian use. The larger cities too have areas assigned to pedestrians, particularly those areas popular with tourists, with examples such as Les Halles and the Marais quarter in Paris around Centre Beaubourg or Covent Garden in London.

3.1
Birmingham, UK. View of part of New Street, previously full of traffic, now part of a pedestrian network crossing the central area.

Paradoxically the larger the city, the fewer pedestrian areas are there in the centre, partly the result of policies which refuse to accept overall traffic reduction. The success of large scale pedestrian areas, in cities such as Hamburg or Munich, depends partly on how animated they are by day and by night and many authorities are encouraging housing to locate in the centre partly to reduce the transport problems as well as encouraging street life. Many old office buildings, for example, with ground level shops, have now had their upper levels converted into flats. Old warehouses are being converted into flats and live-work units are being accepted by authorities. Manchester's inner city population of 200 will have 10,000 by 2002. Young people now want to have affordable homes in or near the city centres. Increased affluence has led to the rebirth of cafes and eating out. Streets teaming with life are generally safer to walk in at night with surveillance by TV cameras overlooking the streets and stations or wherever people congregate, helping reduce crime.

London's Covent Garden is one of London's few pedestrian areas, an important area for tourists. Leicester Square will be connected to Trafalgar Square and to Parliament Square by 2003, and both will be transformed from being traffic roundabouts into squares, accessible for pedestrians. Here the work of 'Space Syntax' has been influential by producing detailed analyses of pedestrian and traffic movement, ensuring that the right design decisions are made, before implementation. London, like many other major cities, has yet to modify its traffic philosophy that traffic routes cannot be changed without gridlock occurring and has for years maximised every available inch of road space for traffic. Trafalgar Square is an important first step in showing that such changes are possible.

Walking conditions in conventional neighbourhoods are, of course, conditioned by the number of vehicles using the road at what speed and how easily and safely they may be crossed. In Delft, Holland a new way of looking at streets was developed in the 1950s in a dense housing area where children were deprived of play space. Subsequently *woonerven* or town yards were created, elaborately landscaped with play areas, and vehicle traffic speeds were reduced through humps or chicanes. Simplified versions of this concept grew across Germany and the movement now known as 'traffic calming' has helped make walking more pleasant and safer in the areas where it has been done. Of particular importance has been the implementation of areas, where communities want them, of 'home zones', where traffic speeds have been reduced to 30 kph (20 mph).

In the UK particular emphasis is now given to areas around and on routes to local schools, to make them safe for children, and to encourage more to walk, rather than be driven. This is partly because traffic authorities have found that traffic congestion at peak hours is exacerbated by the number of mums driving their children to school. At present only one in ten children walk or cycle to school

3.2
Munich, Germany. High-level view of Karlsplatz, the end of the principal pedestrian street, Kaufinger Strasse. Trams (shown at the bottom of the picture) serve nine different routes. The escalators and stairs serve the S Bahn, undergound ticket hall below, combined with a level of shopping and two levels of parking. Courtesy: Bauferat der Landeshauptstadt, Munich.

3.3
Trafalgar Square, London. Proposal, being implemented, showing the effect of closing one side of the square, now a traffic roundabout, to traffic. New wide steps fronting the National Gallery will give access for pedestrians to the square. Architects: Foster and Partners.

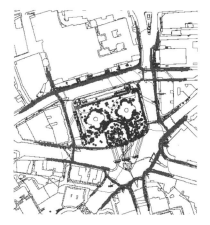

3.4
Trafalgar Square, London. One of many studies made prior to closure of street to traffic on the north side of the square which analyses the effect of street closure and its impact on pedestrian movement. Courtesy: Space Syntax.

in England and the intention is to change this. One system being tried in the UK is 'the walking bus' where children wait at bus stops, are collected by others, and walk in crocodile formation to the school.

A new interest in cycling

There is now an increasing demand by the cycling lobby that a section of each road should be allocated for their use. The extent to which this is done varies between countries, some of which have a tradition of cycling. Now with the blessing of traffic engineers, who have long disregarded cycling as a serious transport system, proper provision for cycling is generally accepted. In Holland, for example, all roads within their cities have cycleways. Action by Green activists in Copenhagen, Denmark resulted in cycleways being provided beside all main roads in the city centre and today around 30 per cent commute by cycle into the centre.

Rail stations in Holland have over 90,000 cycles, parked daily at 80 stations, mostly guarded, and under cover. In Japan, an estimated 1.25 million cycles are parked daily at stations, with multi-level parking being tried on an experimental basis. An office block in Hiroshima has given over its basement to cycle parking. Weather, the terrain and safety are important factors which still deter people from cycling. But in most European countries cycling is steadily increasing.

3.5
Amsterdam, Holland. Cycle parking at the Central Station. Parking is being expanded to 270,000 places in Holland to serve the 30–40 per cent of passengers who cycle to stations. The more remote stations provide secure parking or lockers to assist in preventing theft.

As car ownership grows, road space in cities has become congested for much longer periods and parking has also become increasingly difficult. It is here that public transport has to be quicker and more convenient than driving. In Singapore, drivers now pay to drive into the centre (see p. 43) and this is likely to occur in Western cities within the next 5 years, but will be only politically acceptable, once public transport is improved. The car-free city centre is now a practical proposition (see p. 73). Car-free Sundays are already being tried in Italy and France as a way of reducing pollution levels and to show the public what centres without cars mean, but good public transport is rarely provided at the same time. If public transport was not only efficient but free, it would become increasingly popular.

Part II
Transport and the future city

Chapter 4 Roads in the future city

One of the most critical features of the fabric of a city is the scale of the roads, the width between building faces. With wide roads, infinite variations are possible, pavements can have a generous width with space for trees, stalls and street cafes. Lanes can be provided for cyclists, with minimum width access lanes for servicing. With drop down space for buses and taxis, but with no on-street parking. Space in the centre can be for light rail, for buses or for elevated transit. Alternatively, below street level, along busy corridors, metros can run in shallow tunnels, easily accessible from street level by stairs, escalators and lifts. Smaller roads will be for pedestrians with servicing along them at night. In new development areas laying out this basic structure of wide roads can only be beneficial, provided they do not bring with them more traffic, offering instead great scope for imaginative urban design.

In existing European city centres attempts to alleviate road congestion through building more roads or through road widening has largely ceased, partly because land values are too high, partly because of public opposition. Traffic engineers too – at least the more enlightened ones – now accept that widening only brings in more traffic, although they are still averse to closing a road or reducing a road width in the unshakeable belief that 'traffic must have somewhere to go' (see Trafalgar Square, Figure 3.4). Today road-building and road widening in Europe is largely confined to the suburbs and regions where land is cheap to acquire. This attempts to cater for the rise in cross-city trips although in practice rarely meets the demand for additional road space. This is partly due to development being allowed in areas without consideration being given to the proximity of good public transport.

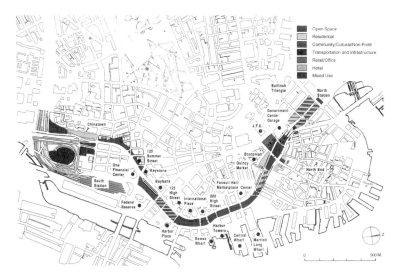

4.1

Boston Central Artery, Massachusetts. Proposed land uses for the Central Artery corridor, once covered by the elevated freeway, to be replaced by a road in a tunnel. Detailed discussions are now being held with local interest groups.

(Figures 4.1–4.5 courtesy: Boston Redevelopment Authority).

4.2

Sketch of one of the possible land uses being discussed – a conservatory with a botanical garden.

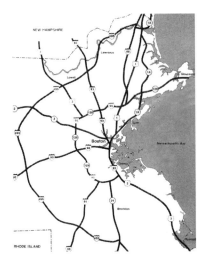

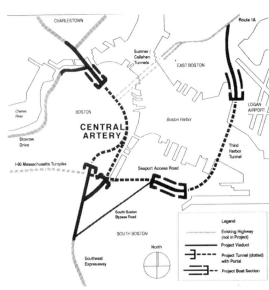

4.3

Road plan of Boston, showing radial routes which converge on the city centre and cross it where around 40 per cent of work trips end.

4.4

Detail plan showing location of the Central Artery to run north–south in a tunnel.

In the United States in the 1950s, a vast programme of urban road building occurred, designed to bring traffic, mostly cars, into and out of the centres. Only in a few cities was the environmental lobby successful in halting the destruction which ensued. For example in San Francisco, the halting of the elevated Embarcadero Freeway and its demolition has now transformed the area into a fine landscaped promenade with a streetcar. This was followed by the halting of the Mount Hood Freeway, in Portland, Oregon, where the population voted instead for the construction of the first section of the light rail Max line with the result that the existing city centre was restored.

In Boston, Massachusetts, a very European city with fine streets and buildings, an eight-lane inner beltway was planned to surround the centre but was stopped by popular demand. Instead a major study held in 1974 called 'The Transportation Review', proposed improving public transport, as well as building a tunnel from what was formerly an elevated freeway called the Central Artery. This six-lane road, built in the 1950s, demolished 36 city blocks and blighted an area of Boston close to the waterfront. Today the eight-lane tunnel and other works being built allow this road to be demolished. Ventilation will be by seven-storeyed buildings, which will also contain offices and parking. This project will be completed in 2004 at a cost of $10.8 billion (around £7,000 million), which costs approximately the same as the Channel Tunnel. Some lanes will be used by electric buses and for car pools.

The ground level space above the tunnel, below the elevated freeway, is now used for car parking. This was the subject of a number of studies, including one by Architects Chan Krieger and Associates (see Figures 4.1, 4.2) which is the preferred solution now being followed. This space above the tunnel, when completed, is now the subject of detailed discussions with local community groups and will be used for special buildings, or small parks (see Figure 4.2). It remains to be seen whether other cities in the US will follow suit, with a move now towards the partial revival of old city centres as 'a place to go', at least for entertainment. There is an increasing interest there in finding ways of improving an environment in cities which had been torn apart by excessive road building.

In 1964 the freeway driving experience was given some credence in Appleyard, Lynch and Meyer's *The View from the Road*. This may have been partly influenced by their experience of driving on the Central Artery in Boston. They concluded that this was 'an exciting way to read the city', that the road should be moved rather than removed, because they felt that this way of moving by car might be what future cities were all about, although they admitted 'a stationary citizen' below it 'would wish it out of sight'.

Whether approaching Boston in the future by tunnel will be similarly exciting remains to be seen. If it is not, will the whole exercise have been worth the effort?

4.5
View of existing elevated freeway built in the 1950s which demolished 36 blocks. Now being replaced by an 8-lane tunnel.

4.6
The view from the road and the buzz from driving downtown along a freeway like this one in Los Angeles continues to excite drivers, and others. Whether driving along these roads in the future, in a tunnel, will be as attractive, remains to be seen.

4.7
Birmingham, UK. A city previously ringed by an inner, elevated ring road which pedestrians had to cross under to reach the city centre in subways. This proposal, now being implemented in stages, shows sections of the ring road demolished to be rebuilt as an urban boulevard crossed by pedestrians at grade level. Courtesy: Birmingham City Council.

Would the money have been better spent on public transport? Probably not in view of the extent to which Boston remains auto-oriented. Although there are plans to provide much improved park-and-ride facilities at the end of extended commuter rail lines, it remains to be seen whether this will be successful in limiting the pressure to increase the present parking limit of 35,000 cars that exist in the centre. Normally enlarging road access, which is what the tunnel is doing, brings more traffic with it. London's Westway, a four-mile elevated road built in the 1960s aimed at the centre, is estimated to have brought 20–30 per cent more traffic into Central London (Plowden, 1980). Hopefully this will not occur in Boston, or it will no longer remain America's foremost 'walking city'.

To sum up, the driving experience of entering or crossing a city by elevated road continues to be one enjoyed by drivers – even if stuck in traffic. Reyner Banham extolled its delights in the context of Los Angeles, in a memorable article 'Roadscape with Rusting Rails' in 1968. But if this means the decimation of a city, or those areas adjacent to roads, then it is clearly no solution. Building around the car culture can be done in two ways: either to build at a low density when land is cheap, like Los Angeles with 60 per cent of land given over for roads and ground-level parking; or to build, at high cost, a new kind of infrastructure, with multi-storeyed parking an essential part of every development. Those cities in Europe which tried to do this, like Birmingham, have since found a way out of this dilemma of dealing with the car and its necessary infrastructure.

In Birmingham, UK, a city of one million people, a notorious inner ring road ran in a tight noose around the city centre with roundabouts at junctions mostly elevated, crossed by pedestrian subways. This was a prime example of postwar car-oriented thinking. Today some of these roads are now being demolished and replaced by surface-level, tree-lined boulevards (see Figure 4.7), laid out with wide pavements and light-controlled crossings for pedestrians. These lead to a new network of fine pedestrian streets (see Figure 3.1) crossing the inner city. Light rail, already running, will increasingly serve the city centre when complete.

Today the car lobby remains powerful, particularly in those countries which employ workers in car manufacturing. Politicians continue to support road-building, perhaps less than before. Motorway scale roads outside the cities will continue to be built, but for how long is difficult to predict. There will always be plans in drawers for more roads waiting to get finance. Plans even now are being made in London, by a private consortium, aiming to build roads in tunnels leading to parking silos under the city centre. The pressure to find ways of driving into cities continues and is likely to do so until the alternatives are good enough.

The intelligent highway

Road congestion has led to continuing research by professionals and academics to find ways to improve the capacity of the networks by using advanced electronics, maximising every inch of road space or junctions, to try and ensure free-flowing traffic. Thus area-wide control of traffic lights will allow for a 'green wave' of traffic which maintains it at a certain speed and keeps it flowing at certain times of the day. One-way streets, for example, or the elimination of turning at junctions, are all measures designed to reduce hold-ups. Traffic flows are now monitored through pads or sensors set in the road and watched via CCTV at central control points so that breakdowns or accidents are quickly identified and remedial measures taken. But with traffic now at saturation point in most cities, still more advanced methods are being studied and tried to keep traffic flowing.

Drivers already listen to traffic conditions on their car radios, to avoid snarl ups. Others may use a device such as the 'Trafficmaster' which will show them on a dashboard screen where traffic congestion is and show alternative routes. The next stages of development will be an interaction between driver and the highway called 'telematics' where a driver on entering his vehicle taps in his required destination on the keyboard of his onboard computer, or simply tells it where he is going and will then be given information on the screen or verbally, showing which route to take to avoid congestion. Once on the road, via the satellite global positioning system, already being marketed, drivers will be told, or shown on a dashboard map, where to make a turn right up to their destination.

Enforcing safe traffic speeds, particularly within built-up areas, can now be possible with the aid of both of these systems. Digital maps can be made which show what traffic speed is permitted within a certain area and the global positioning system will accurately pinpoint the vehicle's position. Once these are both linked to the engine, speeds can be controlled automatically. Trials are already being held in Sweden and Holland although it is too early to judge when a control system of this kind becomes a standard feature in the future.

Drivers in the future will request parking in a certain area, and will be told if it is available and book it in advance, based on a projected time of arrival. Alternatively drivers may be informed when parking is full up and will then be directed to the nearest park-and-ride station – or simply advised to use public transport and leave the car at home. On the road the driver may already use 'cruise control' which will monitor the car's speed without using an accelerator. Hitachi in Japan are road-testing a car with intelligent cruise control with the car's onboard radar adjusting its speed automatically, to keep a safe distance between it and the car in front. All these developments are heavily financed by car manufacturers, anxious to keep cars equipped with the latest on-board gadgetry, in an attempt to make

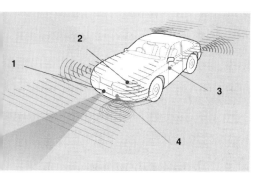

4.8

The future provision of cars with radar devices to make safer driving at close intervals is already being introduced in some vehicles: (1) advanced vehicular gap sensor; (2) nearview sensor; (3) surround view sensor; (4) ground view sensor. Courtesy: Omron Corporation.

4.9
London's Countdown. Real-time information boards are being installed at 4,500 bus stops – around 25 per cent of the total number. The signs show the order of arrival, route destination and minutes to arrival. Around 6,500 buses on 700 routes are being installed with Automatic Vehicle Location systems. Courtesy: Transport for London.

congested roads more tolerable. The Economist Intelligent Unit estimates that 20 per cent of the value of an executive's car based on its electronics system will rise to 30 per cent by 2005 (*Observer*).

Public transport

Some of the technology discussed above is already being used by public transport and by haulage firms. Buses and trams, for example, already use on-board transponders in European cities which turn traffic lights in their favour. Their position can now be tracked within several metres, by global satellite and precisely identified at a central control room. Drivers have on board screens which inform them if they are running on time without using radios. At stops passengers can read on the 'real-time' boards when their vehicle will arrive. This service in London, called 'Countdown', is being fitted to over 6,500 stops on 700 different routes, around 25 per cent of the total number (see Figure 4.9).

Experiments too are being made with road guidance for buses (see p. 133). These can use a single rail set into the roadbed, follow a painted line on the road surface, or by means of magnetic dots in the roadbed. Taxis already use computers and automatic vehicle positioning systems to optimise their trips and reduce wasted travel time. Control centres of haulage firms can identify the position of every vehicle in the fleet particularly useful if there is any concern about theft or of late deliveries due to traffic congestion.

Automated highways

Experiments have been made with automated highways in the United States, on a 20 mile section of the San Diego Freeway (Figure 4.11) as well as in Holland and Japan. Magnetic studs were set at 1 metre intervals along the centre of a lane and cars were equipped with on board magnets which guided them under cruise control and adjusted their speeds and distance between each. The cars ran in fleets – at closer intervals, and higher speeds, than would normally have been possible or safe. In theory automated highways were seen as a new way of maximising flows safely, without the need to build new roads. In practice it was found that while it worked, it was when drivers left the system that the problems arose. The legal aspects, too, meant that to be safe, each vehicle would require to be checked for its suitability, before being allowed to enter the automated highway.

The StarrCar (an acronym for Self Transit Road and Rail Car), developed by William Alden in Massachusetts in the 1960s, is still of interest. Alden proposed

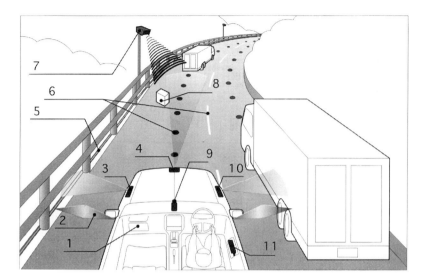

4.10

Future roadside systems will collate a variety of information affecting vehicle flow: (1) information processor; (2) vehicle roadside communication; (3) sensor; (4) laser radar; (5) road infrastructure for vehicle communication; (6) road infrastructure for vehicle control; (7) information collection processing sensor; (8) obstacle; (9) camera; (10) sensor; (11) antenna. Courtesy: Omron.

4.11

San Diego Freeway. Trials made in 1998 with an automated highway. This would permit vehicles to run close together at high speeds controlled by magnetometer dots in the roadbed. The infrastructure costs proved to be too high at present for implementation and on-vehicle collision avoidance systems are considered to be more economic. Courtesy: US Department of Transport.

4.12
Alden's StarrCar, developed by him in the 1960s, was one of the first experiments with a small dual-mode car. This would be driven from homes, along normal roads, or enter a guidance track at stations apart from other traffic. It would then run under electric power to a preselected station where it would leave to enter the normal road system to reach the required destination. Courtesy: William Alden.

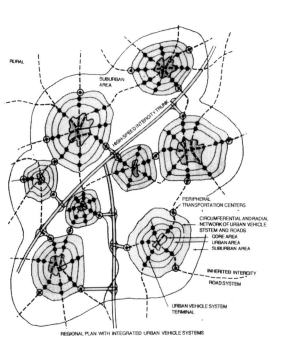

REGIONAL PLAN WITH INTEGRATED URBAN VEHICLE SYSTEMS

and built a small car which would be driven on roads in residential areas for local trips, owned by the city and rented out to householders. For longer trips this would be driven to be checked at an entry-point, running on to a special, narrow two-way lane, situated beside the freeway system. Here the car would accelerate to enter a gap between other cars and run under electric power in platoons with other cars until leaving at the required exit point. Alden, by using a small special vehicle with electric motive power, dealt with pollution as well as the necessity that all cars using the system would be of the same size and, above all, should be checkable for safety. There does seem a case for progressing such an idea further now that the technology has been tried and tested. While such a system could work in lower density areas it would not solve the downtown trips, where vast numbers of small vehicles would be rolling off an automated lane of a freeway into a city centre and would have to be accommodated (see p. 125).

4.13
Cornell Aeronautical Laboratory. A study made by a team working in the 1960s to show how neighbourhoods could be linked by personal rapid transit guideways laid over the existing infrastructure, using a system such as Alden's StarrCar. Courtesy: Cornell Aeronautical Laboratory.

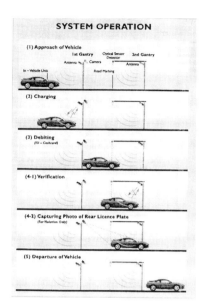

4.14
Singapore. Road pricing, which first started successfully in 1975, initially reduced cars entering at peak hour by 50 per cent. Since 1998 this has been converted from a manual system to one using electronic pricing. Gantries placed at entry points check the validity of cars entering. If invalid, the number plates are filmed automatically and the drivers fined.

4.15
Shows the in-vehicle units now fitted to 97 per cent of vehicles. Drivers pay different prices for the card inserted into it, depending on the type of vehicle. Cards are renewed at banks.
Courtesy: Land Transport Authority.

Paying for road space

One way of reducing the pressure on urban road space in the future is to make drivers pay for using it. For 25 years Singapore has been pricing the roads entering the Central Area, charging vehicles using it at certain times of day for the space they use and the congestion they cause to other vehicles. The idea was first carried out in the form of pilot schemes in Washington DC in 1959 and subsequently in the UK when traffic problems were less acute, but the idea was never put into practice because it was argued then that the technology was not yet available. In 1975 Singapore started tolls for vehicles using simple window stickers read by police at 28 entry points. This was in 1999 and it was superseded by electronic road pricing, which uses a magnetic card which the car owner purchases at a bank and places in an electronic card-holder attached to the front of the vehicle and 'read' from an overhead gantry. Units are deducted automatically for each trip made. Cards are recharged at a bank by drivers when they run out of units, and cameras record the number plate of vehicles with no units on their card and the driver is fined.

Road pricing has been shown in the case of Singapore to be effective in reducing traffic entering a city centre, particularly at peak periods, and the technology allows for variable pricing, not only at entry points, but for the distance driven along certain congested streets. The politics of introducing road pricing into a city are considerable and acceptance by the public is doubtful unless the money realised is devoted to improvements being made to public transport and this being in place before it is implemented. Oslo, Norway, for example, has simple road pricing in its central area and has collected tolls in order to build an underground urban road as well as upgrade its public transport.

Rome has a serious traffic problem with public transport carrying only 40 per cent of total trips, with 2.3 million cars registered and parking for only 1 out of 6 cars. As a result it was decided that a section of the central area should be made a demonstration project, supported by the European Union, for a toll system. The area covered by the toll is around 4 km square and permission to enter is free for residents and for other essential drivers such as doctors who have surgeries in the area. The system will handle around 20,000 vehicle trips at peak periods and consists of four parts comprising:

1. a number of entry points comprising single poles with a device which scans each vehicle entering; the poles have been designed to minimise their visual impact on the historical streets;
2. an onboard box to take a smart card fitted to each car;
3. a computerised communication sub-system which receives details of each vehicle entering or leaving;
4. a central control centre which verifies the status of each vehicle.

Any vehicle which has not been authorised has its number plate photographed automatically and the driver is fined accordingly. The Rome system will be the first fully automated demonstration of road pricing in Europe and is now about to start operation. What is interesting about the system is that it restricts the number of users to those who need to be in the area. Other systems do not do this and so allow any driver who can afford to pay the price to enter.

Detractors of road pricing argue that road pricing will simply allow in those who can afford to pay and that the alternative of simply making certain areas of the city car-free is a simpler solution and preferable. All these solutions seem possible within large cities. Many areas, such as busy shopping streets, would simply be better off without vehicles, apart from possibly trams. In other areas, paying for road space will reduce the vehicle numbers if the toll is sufficiently expensive, make more road space for public transport, for wider pavements and improve walking conditions. Providing free public transport, within the cordon area, paid from the proceeds of road pricing, would help to make it more palatable. Both Seattle and Portland, Oregon, for example, already run free buses in their city centre. Certainly introducing road pricing without first making major improvements to public transport does not seem to be politically acceptable. However, it seems increasingly likely that paying to drive in some areas, at some times of the day, could be normal within the next ten years.

Chapter 5   The future city centre

Most city centres with a strong historical core area are likely to survive and to grow in the future. They will continue to be where businesses want to locate their headquarters and face-to-face contact remains a deciding factor. It is unlikely that even the most sophisticated video-conferencing systems will replace this. The traditional core area will have the capability of offering a rich variety of supporting elements – shops, cultural activities, restaurants and hotels – which cannot be found elsewhere in a defined area and increasingly in the future more people will choose to live there as the quality of the environment improves.

The costs of office space in these central areas will be high and ultimately as land becomes scarce more new air-rights development will be likely to occur over railways where stations provide good access. High-rise development will put pressure both on the need for good quality access by public transport, with a lessening demand for car access as traffic congestion rises. The 'Access Tree' proposed for New York by the Regional Plan Association under Zupan and Pushkarev could yet become a reality, offering as it did – at least in theory – direct access from subway platforms up to offices above. This was intended, almost symbolically, when it was published in 1969, to stress the importance of siting high-rise offices adjacent to subway stations.

With the growth of offices in the core area will come the need for more residential apartments within walking distance. What occurred in 1976 in Toronto could be a model for cities in the future. Here, with the construction of a new underground line, came the opportunity to construct, largely around the stations, 10,000 high-rise apartments for households without children, from which today an estimated 35 per cent of residents walk to work in the Central Area. Similarly

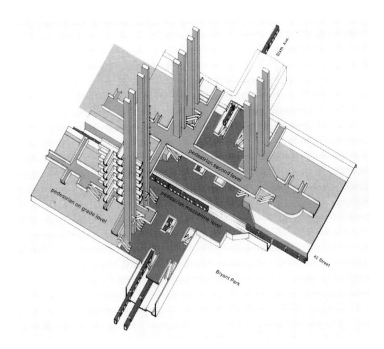

5.1
New York's Regional Plan Study of 1968. Diagram showing the 'Access Tree' concept developed by Okamoto and Williams. This shows how lifts serving high-rise offices could be clustered around a subway station which would be served by a 'mixing chamber' – an elevated concourse, sited above street level, with bridges crossing the surrounding roads. This would give direct access for commuters to the subway platforms below, via the ticket hall, without the need to spill out onto the pavements. Courtesy: Regional Plan Association.

Vancouver between 1986 and 1996 added around 11,000 housing units to its downtown and 37 per cent of all residents walk to work in its West End.

Future city centres, in order to survive, must house more people in the core areas. This will help reduce pressure on the transport system and give life to the centres, particularly at night. There is a real need for affordable living space for 'dinkies' (those with dual income and no kids) who prefer the buzz of a city rather than the peace of a suburb. Developers now want to combine office development with other uses, such as hotels and apartments, with shops and restaurants at ground level, previously never considered economic. There is now a realisation that the environment at street level is important, has an effect on the value of their properties, and that traffic must be tamed if this is to change. Where previously offices were surrounded by a sea of parked cars at ground level (in London's Croydon this still exists) this is now seen to contribute to a hostile environment. Even some Edge Cities in the US are being modified to improve their walking environment.

Future city centres must therefore be planned for a much greater mix of uses than they have in the past. Electronic technology is unlikely to make them obsolete. With more people working from home several days a week, offices in the centres will not only be places for their 'hot desk', but a place where they will meet their fellow workers – if only to compare notes.

Traffic in the future city centre

Dealing with traffic in our future city will be one of the most contentious issues. With the aim to keep the city centre compact and ideally for everything to be within walking distance, roads will be needed to carry only essential traffic. As discussed above (Chapter 4) a basic framework of wide roads or boulevards has the advantage of providing space for essential service vehicles, buses, light rail, cyclists, with possibly shallow underground railways if there is the demand, and of providing generous space for wide, tree-lined pavements. The elimination of vehicular pollution in the city will be the first priority. This is possible through a given period of time during which all vehicles entering the centre or residential neighbourhoods would have to be non-polluting and use either electric power or fuel cells for their engines. Next in priority will be to eliminate congestion on the roads by making drivers pay for road space by road pricing. This will help act as a deterrent to driving into the centre, as will the reduction of on-street parking spaces.

In London around 50 per cent of parking is now in public ownership and could be reassigned for residents' use. Both road-pricing and on-street parking reduction will free road space for public transport, providing space for improving the street environment, through landscaping and widened, tree-lined pavements. The methods of payment to cross a road pricing cordon have been discussed (see p. 43). It will be for the politicians to decide which vehicles pay the tariff and at what hours and whether to apply it to service vehicles to encourage them to make deliveries at off-peak periods.

Residential parking, now on-street, would be phased out with residents offered space within existing multi-storeyed parking buildings, a system already being used in parts of London, taking over space now occupied by commuters. To make this politically palatable will not be easy and it would have to be phased in over a number of years, starting in the most congested residential areas. The street environment would have to be shown to be more attractive, cleaner and safer, with space for children to play. This would be relatively easy to achieve once on-street parking is removed. Copenhagen only achieved this in its centre over a 30-year period.

Some apartment buildings and neighbourhood areas which were made car-free, by common consent, could have a lower rateable value as a result. They could alternatively provide space in their basements for shared cars, provided non-polluting vehicles were used. The only on-street vehicles parked would be the all-electric taxi ranks, smart car hire parks for short-term use, together with some unloading space for deliveries and visitors and for parking cycles. Smart cars would be accessible for holders of smart cards, for short cross-city trips such as carrying baggage or by the disabled who would use them at a reduced rate (see

5.2
The Smart City Bike, developed in Norway. This allows cyclists with a club key to pick them up at racks around the city. Copenhagen has 100 Citybike racks – each with 10 bikes – a simpler system, using coin payment and popular with tourists. Courtesy: Sandnes, Norway.

5.3
A delivery dock costing £7,000, installed experimentally in a new home. This allows for goods to be delivered from outside, opened by a pre-programmed number, and stored in a chilled compartment until being removed by the owner from inside on returning home.
Courtesy: Laing Homes.

p. 114). Main line and principal metro stations would similarly be provided with smart-car parking ranks. Short-term cycle hire points would be available throughout the city centre. Copenhagen has 100 hire Citybike points around the centre, each with ten cycles, which are well-used by tourists for a small fee.

The changes environmentally in a city centre adopting such policies would be considerable. Streets would be less polluted, cleaner and quieter, with relatively few vehicles circulating. They would make walking safer and public transport would be given space to move efficiently. One test area would be undertaken first, to show people what it would be like, rather like introducing the first pedestrian area into a town. It would take considerable political will. The Danes seem to have done it in part of Copenhagen and the results look good.

Handling goods deliveries

Freight vehicles delivering and picking up goods can account for 20 per cent of traffic found today in city centres. In order to reduce this and to help improve the environment it will be important for service trips to and from shops, offices and other buildings to be rationalised and made by a new type of vehicle, better suited to in-city use, of varying sizes, capable of carrying small containers and above all non-polluting. This will require experimenting with the construction, in stages, of transshipment depots sited at the edge of the central area, preferably either over or beside railways and major peripheral roads. These would be run by special delivery firms, open 24 hours a day, and would contain both refrigerated and secure storage areas. The latest goods handling would be used, with smart information systems to identify the incoming and outgoing containerised goods and organise them to reach their destination.

Deliveries   A range of vehicle sizes would be required, all non-polluting, possibly all-electric, or using fuel cell engines, both being quiet enough to allow them to operate at night.

Buildings in the centre which did not employ night staff would be equipped with special delivery hatches to suit the size of containers and opened electronically. The first such delivery hatches are being tried in housing by Laing Homes. Many new buildings would have provision for smaller vehicles to enter, being electric, allowing them to unload directly into showrooms if necessary. By being quiet they would represent no noise problem. Zermatt, Switzerland, has long operated a fleet of all-electric vehicles each designed for different uses, from flat wagons for general goods to small tankers for handling water.

The depots, if large enough, could also be used for storage, freeing space for

5.4
One of a range of small electric vehicles used in Zermatt, Switzerland – a car-free Alpine resort with remote parking and service depot at the edge. The service vehicles used in the town are all electric with each type designed for a specific use, such as builders' trucks, or beer-carrying vehicles. This flat truck is used by the Hotel Europe.

some shops which do not want to expand their expensive downtown space (Plowden, 1980). Such depots are already operating successfully in smaller towns in Holland and there seems no reason why this principle could not be extended gradually to serve larger areas of a city centre. Shops may choose simply to display goods their customers may have seen on the website catalogue but deliver them directly to their homes from out of city warehouses or from factories. This will be a boon for many shoppers using public transport.

In addition, local left-luggage depots or lockers would be sited close to transport stations where customers can store their purchases before leaving by public transport. Hanover already uses a shopping delivery service during the Christmas season where shoppers who have come to the centre by tram leave their packages at a small depot in the city centre. These can either be picked up when they leave, or are delivered to their homes for a small fee. Although this would increase the number of delivery vehicles within local neighbourhoods, road space here is not congested and van drivers using on-board route maps would easily identify the most economic routes to make their trip and so reduce travel distances. At the homes, the built-in delivery hatch mentioned above would be invaluable.

These are some of the methods which in the future could help alleviate the present chaos experienced in cities by delivery vehicles. Gronigen in Holland has already experimented with the depot idea successfully. The organisations already exist, such as those thousands of dairies in England who deliver a bottle of fresh milk daily on every doorstep by electric van. Only the political will is required to experiment with such systems to show the advantages to retailers, offices and residents.

Future goods handling   In new development, such as sub-centres, multi-use service tunnels carrying cables, pipes and drainage below roads are already standard practice. These would easily be able to include pneumatic tube systems to handle refuse and smaller deliveries. Disneyworld Florida uses the Swedish Centrasug system to remove refuse to a central depot for recycling. London, for example, has for long used a small-scale automatic, driverless underground railway to carry mail across the city from the central mail sorting office to a main line station. A recent proposal made by the architect Kisho Kurokawa was to have a ring tunnel below Tokyo to handle goods. Such systems in the long term will prove economic and with the technology already invented it is likely that there will be changes in the field of goods handling in city centres in the next 25 years.

Walking in the future city centre

The popularity of the environment in the new era of well-designed out-of-town shopping malls shows that future cities will have to provide for similar levels of comfort in their shopping areas, if they are to survive. So far only the smaller cities in Germany, like Hamburg or Munich, have created highly successful centres, partly because they have been able to deal more readily with their traffic, creating well-used, and popular pedestrian areas. In large cities like London and Paris, this has hardly begun. It is perhaps significant that one of the most popular areas for tourists to shop in Paris at weekends is now the underground shopping mall, attached to the Louvre, away from traffic and mostly artificially lit.

Cold-weather cities   In cities where winter conditions prevail for six months in the year as in Canada, or in hot humid cities like Hong Kong or Singapore, protection against weather becomes important. In the cold cities, like Montreal or Toronto, the solution adopted has been to push pedestrians into a warren of underground shopping passageways linked with the metro stations, rightly criticised for the lack of orientation afforded to the users (Sorkin, 1992). The alternatives, in Calgary or Minneapolis, of building elevated bridges linking the centres of city blocks appears, at least superficially, to have been more successful. However, both levels, underground or elevated, take pedestrians away from the ground level, making the streets dead. Both also end up being policed areas, to keep out the down at heel, at the same time being closed at night.

Arcaded streets   The surface level solution of arcaded or canopied pavements is both flexible and more sympathetic to accommodate change. It simply requires planning control to require that all new buildings along certain street frontages provide space for covering the pavement by some means. In Adelaide, South Australia, for example, where there can be heavy rain in winter, development in Rundle Mall in the centre requires shops to provide canopies over part of the pavement. Rainy weather, in fact, was found in a study for New York to reduce pedestrian traffic within the shopping streets by as much as 30 per cent. The alternative to building arcades or canopies could be to roof over a shopping street once it is freed from traffic. One example of this is Leeds, England, which already had three arcaded streets and where an additional street has been simply roofed over. Surface-level arcades such as these avoid the necessity of creating mega redevelopment projects which might take years to achieve and require the permission of all building owners on the street. By remaining part of the public thoroughfare they avoid being policed by security men and, unlike the enclosed malls, remain open at night.

5.5
Leeds, UK. A newly covered existing street, where the glass canopy is supported away from the existing buildings on free-standing columns, in a city with three other street arcades. Architect: Derek Latham.

Covered streets   Simple, covered shopping streets, often quite modest in scale, exist in all towns and cities in Japan, where it can rain heavily. Hiroshima, for example, has a network of small, covered streets radiating from the central station, brilliantly lit, often with only single storeyed shops on either side. These are made to look taller through false façades, whose owners are happy to contribute to construction costs for the 'roof', which binds together the shops into a 'mall'. In the past these were a fire hazard, but with today's technology the evacuation of smoke in an emergency can be implemented by careful design. Weather protection at transport interchanges is also important, for example at stops between bus and light rail. This is often provided for in suburban locations in France and is environmentally easier to handle there than in the city centre. The examples of Pirmil station serving the light rail and bus interchange in Nantes (see Figure 8.88) or the Corum station in Montpellier (see p. 149) show how a simple high-level roof provides adequate protection against rain, or hot sun, and is also used to create a focal point for the area.

Covered cities   Ideas for covering whole city centres with a dome were made by Buckminster Fuller in a sketch for Manhattan and in 1967 by Frei Otto (see p. 52) with his feasibility study for an Antarctic City (see Figure 5.6) under a single dome 2 km in diameter. Goods movement would be underground and pedestrian movement under the dome would be within a traffic free area, aided by moving pavements entering through an air lock from the parking garage outside.

Weather protection is just one of the technical problems which should be considered in planning for improved walking conditions in any future city – and it is a problem that *has* to be solved if tomorrow's city centres are to continue to attract people to them.

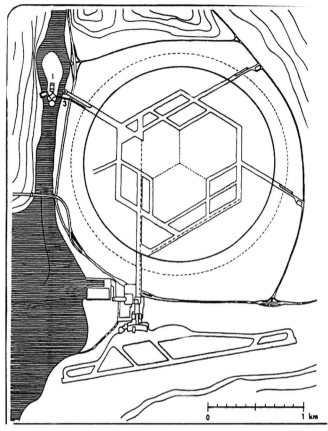

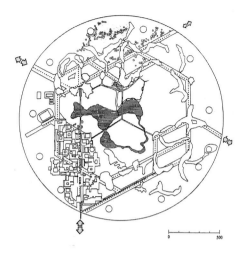

5.7
Plan at high level showing internal layout with a network of moving pavements and ski lifts within the 2 km diameter dome. Courtesy: Frei Otto with Ewald Bubner.

5.6
Project for a covered city in the Antarctic for 20,000 people made in the 1960s. Plan showing expressways outside the dome that link the harbour and the airport to the parking garage situated outside. From here runs a high-speed moving pavement system through the air lock connecting the administration and the housing.

5.8
Views of the model outside the air-supported dome.

Chapter 6 Transport availability in city centres

Underground systems

Metros run today in 84 cities in the world and have a capacity of 20–40,000 people an hour in each direction at average speeds of around 30 kph (20 mph), running normally underground across the city centre. The depth of the line will depend on such factors as soil conditions or the street layout. Where roads are wide, metros can be built quickly, using cut and cover construction and station platforms around 10 m below street level are readily accessible served by stairs, escalators and lifts. Deep tunnelled tube lines, often 20 m down, are normally served by inclined escalators and lifts and mean that station platforms take longer to reach (see also p. 27). Stations now normally require lift access for the disabled, which is also a boon for pushchair users. Train frequency in new driverless systems is high, with trains running at intervals of around two minutes, an important factor in reducing travel times.

If ground level construction sites are available, depending on the soil conditions, box construction for stations can be cheaper than tunnelling. The two stations shown, Bilbao's Sariko with a 50 m long platform, or Copenhagen's new station in the centre, with a 40 m platform, serve short trains, compared to London's tube platforms which average 120 m long. The sections illustrate how light can be brought down to platform level and Copenhagen's station shown will provide a new square at street level.

Metros are still prohibitively costly and slow to build compared with surface level or elevated systems. Few cities in the future are likely to be able to afford them due to their high cost, or require systems that carry such large numbers of

6.1
Bilbao Metro, Spain. Sariko station showing the escalators rising from the mezzanine over the tracks to the ground-level ticket hall from which lifts descend directly to platform level. Architects: Norman Foster and Partners.

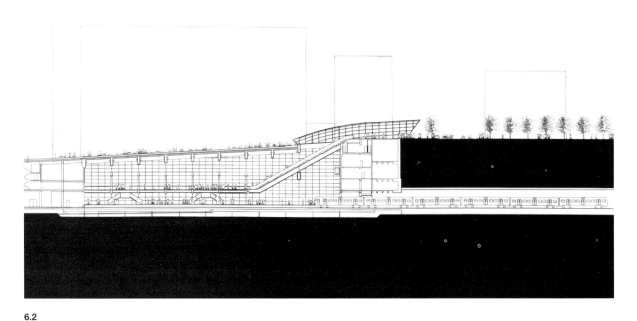

6.2
Long section showing glass roof over ticket hall on right with escalators down to mezzanine level from which stairs descended to the 50 m long platforms. Walls are lined with precast concrete panels and there is no advertising.

6.3
Sariko station entrance.

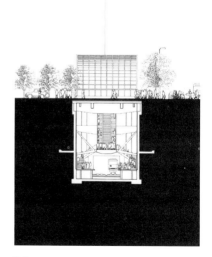

6.4
Cross section through Sariko station built in
box construction. The intermediate walkway is
combined with bracing to help brace the sides
of the box.

6.5
Bilbao Metro, one of many glazed entrances to stations, known locally as 'Fosteritos'.

people along a single corridor. Small scale, low-capacity lines, capable of carrying 20,000 passengers an hour or less in each direction, are more likely to benefit the travel needs of a city. Copenhagen's metro, or the Val systems built in Lille and Toulouse, both small-scale metros, may prove to be more useful systems, although they still cost around 8–10 times more than surface light rail. Those cities which already have metros frequently expand them, regardless of cost, partly because they have management and staff already available to operate and maintain them. However, the concept of using light rail as an extension of a metro, as discussed below, appears to be a preferable solution.

The case for surface light rail

Light rail (see also p. 13) systems, formerly known as trams, are now successfully animating pedestrian areas, where traffic has been removed. In city centres in Strasbourg and Grenoble, light rail has been well-integrated into the streets and squares with vehicular traffic routes redesigned to allow room for light rail to run unimpeded, with priority at all light-controlled junctions. Overall travel speeds of light rail, at 17–21 kph (11–13 mph), is slower than an average metro, which can average 30 kph (20 mph), or a system like Vancouver's Skytrain (see below) at 47 kph (29 mph). Their advantage is one of ease of access, for passengers, as well as the benefits they can bring to the street environment. To avoid over-lengthy travel times (many people will be standing), smaller cities do not normally extend light rail lines beyond a length of 10 km (6 miles) although Lyons is an exception with its new line almost doubling this length.

Light rail is frequently said to be around seven times less expensive than either underground or elevated systems, although these figures ignore the cost of upgrading the streets through which they pass. The recent French examples where this has been done are important and discussed further (see p. 142). In new development areas, light rail has the possibility of shaping the design of buildings around stations, to form focal points along a line (see p. 62). In large cities it can be used in conjunction with a metro or railway lines acting either to relieve an existing overloaded line or to act as a feeder to the station. London is now planning two new light rail lines which will both act as feeder systems to the underground.

A future for elevated systems

In Asian cities like Bangkok or Tokyo, along corridors where there is little apparent concern for the street environment and where conservation areas do not exist,

6.7
View below central interchange station in Bangkok, where two lines cross at right angles. Something of Ridley Scott's film *Blade Runner* when viewed from ground level.

6.6
Bangkok's 23 km long elevated railway opened in 1999 with two lines intersecting in the centre running above densely trafficked roads where speeds are around 10 kph (6 mph). This view shows a typical station and the traffic below. Courtesy: Parsons Brinckerhof.

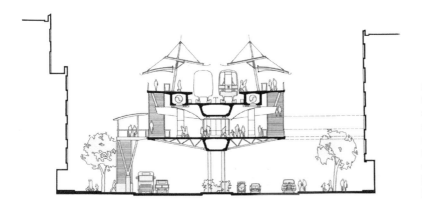

6.8
Cross section through station in Bangkok showing mezzanine ticket hall below the platform level with future bridges over roads connecting into new development alongside. Station roofs are intended to provide cross ventilation. The original stairs to street level are being replaced by escalators. Courtesy: Building Design Partnership.

elevated systems of transport, heavy metros, monorails or light rail have been built, having considerable visual impact on the streets over which they run. However the gain in travel times compared with surface level transport, and the fact that people like to ride on them, appears to outweigh their visual impact.

Bangkok, has completed a privately funded elevated transit system, running in two directions, 23 km (14 miles) long across the centre, with an interchange station at the crossing point. Its construction period of around four years was less than half the time it will take to build an underground in a city with a high water table (see Figure 6.6). The system has a capacity of 22,000 passengers an hour in each direction at a maximum speed of 80 kph (50 mph). Travelling above street level traffic a journey can take 15 minutes which at street level can take two hours. The 23 elevated stations, all naturally ventilated, are designed to serve large numbers of people with ticket halls at mezzanine level that can in the future be connected by bridges into new developments on either side. While the effect below a station has something of Ridley Scott's downtown in his film *Blade Runner* (see Figure 6.7), this does not appear to be problematic for the inhabitants, except that fares are too high to be affordable.

In Kuala Lumpur, a monorail being built across the centre runs partly through an historic area over narrow streets. This is appreciated by one eminent local architect, 'because it gives shade to the street'. Monorails project an image of future transport, at least to members of the public, compared to other systems, using conventional rail track, perhaps partly because of the aerodynamic shape often given to the vehicles. The twin beams of a two-way monorail allow some light between them but are disliked by transport operators because of the difficult and slow 'switching' between lines, which requires an elaborate horizontal mechanism to turn the track.

In Seattle, the only public monorail operating in North America, a 2 km long system was built in 1962, to connect the World's Fair Expo site with downtown. Initially this met with opposition from property owners along its route, with 40 per cent of those questioned saying that their property value had decreased although at the time of the survey 32 per cent felt no change. It is understood that this was solved later, through compensation. The Museum of Contemporary Music by architect Frank Gehry wraps around the existing monorail track (see cover photo). The Seattle monorail today continues to be regarded as something of a symbol of progress for that city. It carries over 1.6 million people a year, mostly tourists, and serious efforts are being made by its supporters, with some 20,000 signatures, for it to be extended to serve the city, instead of the light rail system now under study.

In Tokyo, a new elevated heavy rail system, the Waterfront Transit, has now been completed, running in a loop, with 12 new stations to serve land reclaimed from Tokyo Bay, which will now be developed. The system, which looks extremely

6.9
Disney World, Florida. View of the 20th century hotel, served by a full-scale two-way monorail running through its main lobby at second floor level, with station platforms from which lifts can be taken to any level. The free system runs in a loop around the development linking with another hotel, the main car parking area and the Theme Park.

6.10
Seattle, Washington. The 1.6 km long monorail
connecting the World's Fair site with the city
centre was built in 1961. It is shown here
running through a section of the new
Experience Music Project. Photo: Stanley
Smith/EMP.

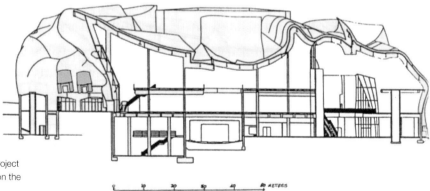

6.11
Section through the Experience Music Project
with the two-way monorail track shown on the
left. Courtesy: Frank Gehry, Architect.

heavy in scale, is presumably designed to be earthquake-proof, and has been conceptually designed, following three principles, 'Human, Fresh and High Tech'. It remains to be seen whether the stations, which have already been completed, can be successfully integrated into the new development area.

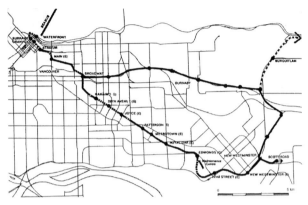

6.13
Vancouver, British Columbia. Plan showing 40 km (25 mile) long Skytrain, which runs largely elevated through the suburbs and in a tunnel in the centre. The most recent 21 km (13 mile) long section is shown at the top, completing the loop.

6.12
Views of the precast Skyway guideway in Vancouver, built in three-metre lengths and post-stressed. Showing columns situated alongside or in the centre of the main roads with columns at 37m centres. Photo: Ron Simpson.

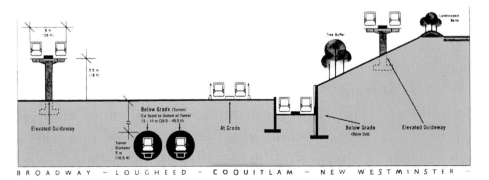

6.14
Sections showing alternative locations for Skytrain track. Being driverless, this requires a fully segregated track. Skytrain runs elevated, within residential areas, entering the city centre in a tunnel. Courtesy: Rapid Transit Project 2000 Ltd.

In Vancouver, British Columbia, a transport plan was developed in 1971 to meet public opposition to freeway construction. Part of this plan was to upgrade its bus and trolley bus fleet, as well as build along a 21 km (13 mile) long corridor, the first leg of an elevated and advanced system called Skytrain. Today the second leg of the system is now being completed to form a continuous loop covering much of the residential area (see Figure 6.13). The system with a capacity of 7,500 people an hour in each direction has average service speeds of 47 kph (29 mph). Driverless vehicles running at two-minute intervals, driven by advanced linear motor with no moving parts, will run in a prefabricated concrete track on columns spanning 35 m. The second stage has been erected in 18 months on the centre, or beside, wide main roads in the suburbs (see Figure 6.12) where there is no overshadowing of adjacent buildings and the line runs underground into the central area in a tunnel. There was considerable opposition to the high cost of this second stage of Skytrain, with many believing that light rail would cost much less, as well as provide a comparable service which could be easily extended.

London's Docklands light rail system (DLR) started as a 8 km (5 mile) long system elevated automated transit system that could be cheaply built, and running within five years, to help give a forward-thinking image to the new developing areas. Today the DLR has been extended into a 26 km (16 mile) long system, crossing the Thames into south London, with extensions planned to connect to the City Airport and beyond. Part of the system, out of the City, runs in a tunnel, the remainder is elevated, crossing the former docks, and supported on elegant arched beams. Where it runs close to housing areas, stringent tests are made annually to assess the noise levels, which are reduced by providing noise barriers beside the tracks. The DLR station at Canary Wharf (see p. 81) sandwiched between office façades, has two platforms connecting directly into the shopping area. Other stations on the line are similarly being connected to the development, serving the new East London University (see p. 62), with two stations serving a new exhibition centre. The DLR at Canary Wharf, however, fails to connect directly with the new Jubilee Line underground station, an idea rejected at the planning stage because it was thought there would be 'no demand for interchange'.

Overhead systems of transport, viewed from below, are intrusive, the stations even more so. They either require to be planned along wide corridors, such as has even been done in Vancouver (see Figure 6.12) which makes stations less accessible, or require buildings adjacent to their tracks to be soundproofed, in which practice is rarely done. However, future cities are increasingly likely to use elevated transit, because it is cheaper than tunnelling, and because they can be built to cause minimal interference with traffic at ground level. Rarely can it be said that their insertion into an existing area will actually 'improve' the environment through which they pass.

6.15
London's Docklands Light Railway (DLR). High-level view showing station serving first phase of the new University of London campus. The roundabout, now redundant, is a relic of the original traffic plan for the area but had to be retained.

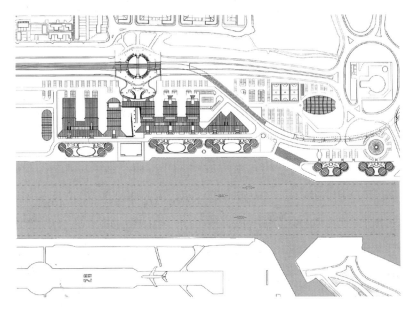

6.16
Plan of university campus showing DLR station relating to entrance plaza. Architect: Edward Cullinan.

6.17
View of bridge serving DLR platforms and connecting them with the university courtyard.

6.18 *facing page*
Greenwich, London. High-level view showing Docklands at top left with the DLR extension connecting to south London, running below the River Thames in tunnel. The elevated line shown connects to Lewisham and was constructed in three years, carrying around one million passengers a month. Photo courtesy: Chorley & Hanford.

6.19
Small monorail running above the International Garden Exhibition in Stuttgart. Driverless trains carry 60 people, all seated, giving a capacity of 3,500 people/hour at a speed of 18 kph (11 mph). Courtesy: Intamin Transportation.

Small monorails

Small-scale monorails have proved to be popular at theme parks and World's Fairs and, in spite of attempts to introduce them into cities to be part of the public transport system, there are few examples where this has been done. Their capacities are around 5,000 people an hour in each direction, often considered by transport operators as being too low. The systems are also criticised as being not robust enough to deal with handling large numbers of people over many years, although this simply means constructing the system, to a higher standard. There are areas of any city where systems of small monorails would be both profitable and great fun for tourists and residents. Sydney, Australia, constructed a 3 km monorail loop in 1988, passing through its centre to link with Darling Harbour, a renewal project. In spite of attempts by the heritage lobby to have it demolished – it does admittedly cross in front of several fine buildings – the system is still running today, is popular with tourists and now interchanges with a light rail extension.

Pedestrian systems

Within large new development areas of cities, distances beyond 500 m may be too great to walk without an alternative mode of transport. The analogy of the horizontal lift could be made here. Multi-level buildings rely on lifts, with around 4–5 per cent of office building costs set aside for their provision. Similarly large areas of development, which have to be crossed on foot, for example, from the main generators of movement, such as stations, need systems of transport and this should be considered and budgeted for at the planning stage. Here will be an opportunity to use systems such as moving pavements, long discussed by futurists like H.G. Wells in 1900 in his book *When the Sleeper Awakes* as the way we would be moving by the year 2000 (Richards, 1966). Moving pavements used at airports help alleviate the tedium of walking out to remote lounges, and walking distances in excess of 500 m are the norm. Some airports, like London's Heathrow, now advise passengers to allow 15 minutes to reach some remote lounges.

Moving pavements have a major advantage over other systems by being able to be built incrementally, in lengths of 100 m and longer. Singapore's new business centre Marina South, which is being planned (see p. 65), covers a 2 sq. km area and will consist of an elevated deck, at second-floor level, which will serve the various office towers. Pedestrian movement will be within air-conditioned shopping malls, on foot, aided by a network of 100 m long moving pavements, with breaks between each, to give access to the office lobbies as well as allow them to be

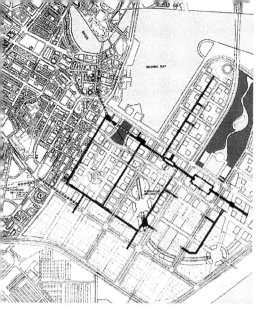

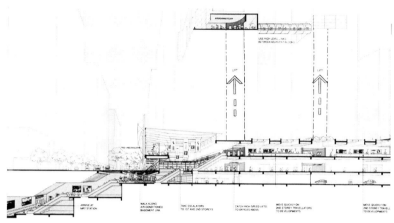

Direct connection from MRT/LRT and interceptor car parks to developments

6.20
Singapore's new downtown, planned to be on reclaimed land around Marina Bay. Plan of development at deck level shows how a network of moving pavements will serve the pedestrian malls, connected by escalator to the two underground stations (MRT).

6.21
Section through part of the development with MRT station at low left. On the second floor deck level moving pavements will run in short lengths of around 100 m, giving access to office lobbies.

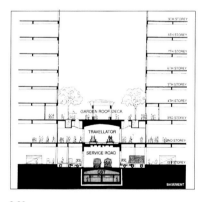

6.23
Cross section through typical street between office blocks with roof garden, moving pavements below running at deck level with service traffic at ground level, and combined services tunnel below street. Courtesy: Urban Redevelopment Authority.

6.22
Sketch showing entrance lobby to high-rise offices at deck level with moving pavements at left and right broken at this point to form an entrance landing to the offices.

crossed. The development will be in stages to allow the systems to be installed as the walking distances from the two metro stations serving the development increase. Further transport by bus and light rail will be on the road system below the deck, linked by escalator and lifts.

In future city centres, along streets, where ideally vehicular traffic has been removed, moving pavements could run in 100–150 m long sections, the length of each city block. A study was made for the Department of Transport in South Australia in 1978 (see Figures 6.24, 6.25, 6.26) by the author, commissioned by the Dunlop Company, to study how moving pavements in Adelaide could help link the main railway station with the centre. Following discussions with the police, fire and traffic authorities, the most practical level and position to run them, because traffic had to be retained, was the central reservation of the street with access from the street crossings at each block junction. Weather protection was required due to the often very wet conditions that prevail in the winter months and the problems of keeping water out of the driving motors.

Moving pavements, elevated above streets, require escalators and lifts for access. A fine example of this is a system built to serve the Hanover Fair of 2000 where moving pavements run within a glazed tube across an existing railway (see pp. 108–110) linking the station with the exhibition grounds. Alternatively moving pavements can run below streets, within subways. This occurs around Shinjuku Station in Tokyo, where over 2 million passengers a day are handled at the station and this has extended the catchment of the station. Paris already has seven moving pavements operating underground at three interchange stations within subways. With the high cost of underground metro stations, moving pavements can extend a station's catchment, and increase the number of entrances over a wider area.

Moving pavements at present suffer by being too slow – at 40 m/minute, half walking speed – and expensive for what they achieve. The new high-speed moving pavement systems being developed in Japan, which are reputed to be no more expensive, will be three times faster, accelerating at up to 120 m/minute (see pp. 111, 112). If these prove to be popular, they will be useful at those points in city centres for distances of up to 500 m and over, serving high-capacity transport systems such as metros, where the dispersal of large number of people is required.

6.24
Adelaide, South Australia, 1978. Study of moving pavements for the Dunlop Company made for the Director General of Transport. Aimed at finding ways of using them in the central area to link the Central Business District with the main line station. View of King William Street with moving pavements running under cover in central reservation.

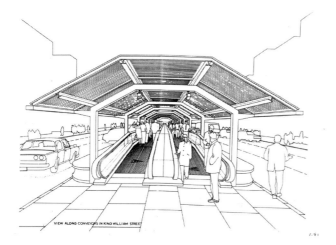

6.25
Detail showing moving pavement ramping up from central island, linked to surrounding pavements at each block junction. This allows passengers to travel slightly raised above traffic level to improve view and travel clear of fumes. Architect: Brian Richards. Consulting engineers: Ove Arup and Partners.

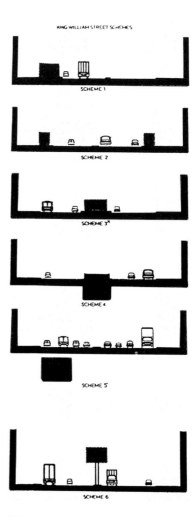

6.26
Sections show alternative locations for moving pavements in King William Street. Scheme 3 proved to be the most practical solution, to run in block lengths, accessible at corner street crossings.

6.27
Tokyo, Japan. Proposal made in 1970 for Shinjuku, a major transport
interchange. Moving pavements were to run elevated in air-conditioned
tubes, connecting elevated platforms at junctions. These would distribute
passengers from the main line station above traffic to offices.

6.28
View from inside the elevated air-conditioned tube.

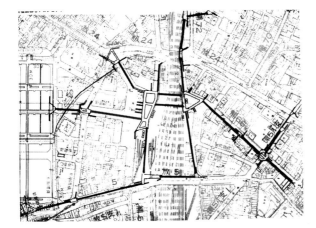

6.29
Plan showing location of elevated system based on that used at the
World's Fair in Osaka. Architect: Koichi Sone.

Vehicles in future city centres

Over the years city centre road space has become increasingly cluttered with vehicles, both stationary and moving. This must change if streets are to be made safer and more pleasant places to walk. With the increasing numbers of people wanting to return to live in city centres and their demand for a better environment, this too could encourage changes to take place.

A road pricing cordon around the Central Area of a city (see Figure 6.30) will help reduce the number of vehicles entering (the estimated figure for London is a 20 per cent reduction). Yet it will not reduce the number of vehicles on the roads sufficiently to improve the street environment and additional changes are necessary. Higher parking charges already deter some people driving into a centre, but there will always be those who will pay, and can afford to, regardless of cost. If we really want to improve a city's streets then measures have to be introduced which will free them from excessive traffic, as well as the tyranny of kerbside parking.

The first priority will be on those streets used by buses. These streets would be turned into transit malls, as well as being made pleasant places to walk or to cycle, with wider pavements where cafes occur, and adequate space for tree planting and for well-designed bus stops. Along key routes, light rail will be required as an alternative to buses. However, light rail, by requiring its own right of way, will also require the streetscape to be redesigned. In some cases the street will be made pedestrian-only, with new paving and street furniture and the clutter of irrelevant signs removed along the route. This would follow the best examples already found in cities like Grenoble, France, where one-third of the total costs of the light rail system was spent in repaving streets and on making environmental improvements to the centre (see p. 142).

Clean air   Road transport at present causes a high proportion of pollution in cities and is strongly linked to both acute and chronic respiratory illnesses, being responsible for around 75 per cent of particulate and nitrogen dioxide emissions in London. Here, of the 180,000 vehicles entering the Central London cordon daily, 65 per cent are cars and 19 per cent are goods vehicles. Older cars, together with diesel vehicles such as taxis and goods vehicles, are the worst offenders.

Air monitoring already shows where the problem areas are and where it will be necessary for 'dirty' vehicles to be phased out. Camden, for example, following research into air pollution levels, is considering that all old taxis operating within their area change to petrol and no longer use diesel fuel. With the development of cheaper fuel cell engines (see p. 140) within the next four years, it should be possible for all delivery vehicles, taxis and buses to use this completely non-polluting source of power, or use hybrid battery-electric power.

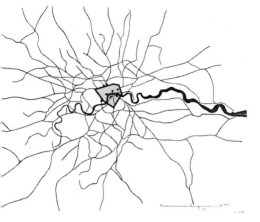

6.30
Central London plan showing the size of the central area proposed to be within the road-pricing cordon and which measures around 5.5 km sq. This is now entered by 180,000 vehicles a day of which 65 per cent are cars and 19 per cent are goods vehicles. Road pricing may reduce this by 20 per cent and is intended to produce revenue for improved public transport.

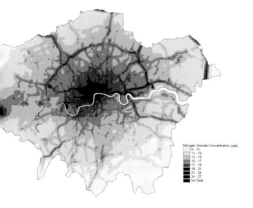

6.31
Map showing present pollution levels in Central London. Although now dropping due to cleaner engines, old diesel taxis and heavy goods vehicles remain the worst offenders and may be phased out. Courtesy: Cambridge Environmental Research Consultants Ltd.

6.32
London. Fountains in the courtyard of Somerset House. One of the first public spaces in the city to be made for 60 years. Formerly used as a car park by income tax inspectors. Architects: Jeremy Dixon and Edward Jones.

Eventually a ban on all vehicles with polluting engines, including cars, in the city centre may be introduced.

Dealing with cars   The present situation of streets being lined with parked cars could gradually be eliminated. This would start with those streets where public transport would run. Buses serving commuters and shoppers, followed by light rail, would be given room to move efficiently and so eliminate, gradually, the need for on-street parking. At present retailers frequently claim that on-street parking is essential for them, if their shops are to survive. The combination of free buses for shoppers on convenient routes near the shops, linked to tube and rail stations, and light rail running along the principal shopping streets should help reduce, or even eliminate, the demand for shoppers' parking on the street.

On-street residential parking could also be gradually eliminated. Residents could instead use the multi-level parking found in every city, but often used by commuters. These could be acquired by the city, if in private ownership, offering parking space for car clubs, local residents and finally any spare space for short-wait visitors. London's Butler's Wharf already has started this trend, by constructing new parking buildings, with upper floors assigned for local residents, who are prepared to pay a fee of £2,000 a year – nearly 20 times the cost of on-street parking, which has now been largely removed.

The developers of office buildings, in the past, were frequently required to provide parking space for their office staff. Once road pricing is introduced, there may be less demand for their use by their staff, many of whom will have changed from driving in to taking public transport. This has already occurred in the City of London since their 'ring of steel' cordon was introduced. This was done, following a terrorist attack reducing the number of entry points, into the City to five, making driving in so difficult that it has reduced the demand for parking. The gradual elimination of on-street parking could bring with it real environmental advantages, depending on the area. It will, for example, enable road widths to be reduced, allowing room for cycle lanes. Within residential areas it will allow more space for trees, for wider pavements and landscaping. Some streets would be traffic-free, creating the *woonerfs* or town yards found in central Berlin, creating areas where children are safe to run about and to cycle safely. The city centre of Copenhagen, for example, over a period of 30 years has expanded the area called Stroget to over three times its original size, which now covers an area of 7 hectare. Areas where cars were previously parked were studied section by section by a team of planners and alternatives were produced for discussion with the residents, before changes were made. The end result is a fine tribute to the patience and single-mindedness of the many people involved.

Some new housing being built in Central London, for example, is now car-free (see p. 98). In New York's Manhattan large numbers of residents, rich and poor, live in apartment buildings without cars, from choice, but hire them as the need arises. Car clubs, notably in Switzerland and Germany (see p. 122) already encourage people to give up their cars, hiring them when needed. Car clubs have already started in Britain in Leeds, Edinburgh and Oxford. On-street parking lay-bys would be provided on each block, for delivery vehicle use. Ranks for short-term electric hire cars, at regular intervals (see p. 114) would serve people needing a vehicle for carrying goods over short distances, for disabled drivers, or for night-time use. These hire vehicles would be returned to their original stand for recharging when no longer required. Hire cycles, popular with tourists in Copenhagen, could be available at racks largely for the use of tourists. Taxi ranks at rail or metro stations, as occurs in Paris, would reduce the need for the present cruising which occurs to pick up fares.

Deliveries   Delivery and goods vehicles would pay a high price to enter the cordon area at peak hours, to encourage off-peak or night-time use. Shops, offices and housing would be encouraged to install large editions of the new refrigerated delivery hatches (see Figure 5.2) now being tried. This would help simplify night-time deliveries and reduce the need for extra staff. In the long term, trans-shipment depots (see p. 49) would be situated near railway stations, or adjacent to major roads. To eliminate vehicles crossing the centre the sector principle would be adopted. This has been in use since 1970 in Gothenburg, Sweden (see Figure 6.33) and is now common practice in many town and cities with ring roads. Here turnings into the cordon area, off the perimeter ring road, are clearly labelled, to make it easy for vans, taxis and other vehicles to identify their correct entry-point to reach a specific area. These vehicles having completed their trip return on to the ring road and thus cross-centre movement is avoided. Only the light rail system crosses the sectors. The efficiency of such a system will depend on the capacity of the ring road and on how this road can be confined to essential traffic.

Taxis, for example, or car-borne visitors to an hotel, enter at a clearly signed point on the perimeter road and use the existing road network, which would be relatively traffic-free to reach their required destination. This system has been common practice for many years in pedestrianised centres in smaller towns in Europe. Many, for example, list at the entry points, the names of the hotels and sign the junctions accordingly. In larger cities this is more difficult, but already hire cars in the US have on-board telematics at a slightly higher charge. This is likely to be standard equipment in many cars soon, informing a driver verbally of the appropriate turning to reach a specific destination or if there is any parking available or, if not, where to find it.

These are some of the ideas and strategies which could occur before and after

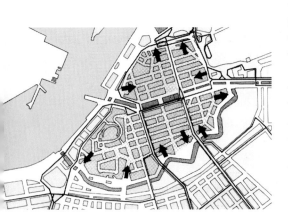

6.33
Gothenburg, Sweden. Central area traffic plan, adopted in 1970, designed to stop cross-city vehicle movement. This divides the centre into five sectors, with each sector entered from the peripheral road, with only trams allowed to cross the centre between the zones. Courtesy: City of Gothenburg.

road pricing is introduced into a city. Financing them would be at least partly met from the income from the tolls, estimated in the case of London to be around £200 million per year. Apart from the shoppers' free buses, it should not be necessary to subsidise the running of either light rail or commuter buses. Instead funds should be set aside every year for environmental improvements to the streets, such as traffic calming, pavement widening and tree planting. These cost large amounts of money, both to build and to maintain.

A car-free London   Many of the ideas discussed above were incorporated in the author's submission in the Car-free London Competition held in 1998 (see p. 74), organised by the Architecture Foundation (which received an honorary mention). The drawings showed how a range of improvements could be implemented, over an eight-year period (possibly an over-optimistic span), required for the legislation and construction time to build at least two tram lines across the Central Area, enclosed by the road pricing cordon. Improving surface level transport would be the first priority, with a new fleet of articulated low-floor buses to serve commuters, to complement an overloaded tube system. Singapore, for example, introduced 90 new buses, when it first started road pricing in 1975. A fleet of single-decker shoppers' free buses, with wide doors and low-floored, would serve internal movement and help to keep shopping an attractive activity. Both Seattle and Portland, Oregon have free bus travel in their centres. Denver, on its one-mile-long mall also runs free specially designed wide-door shoppers' buses.

Deliveries by non-polluting vehicles, at off-peak periods, with access into each zone have been discussed. Limited on-street parking for visitors would be on streets not used by buses. Frequent short-term car hire points would be on alternate blocks. Multi-storeyed car parks (see sketch, Figure 6.38) would be increasingly used by residents and commuter parking phased out. Finally the key to the proposal would be a light rail system, on largely pedestrian-only streets, running north–south and east–west. This would subdivide the centre, with the only streets crossing the lines limited to essential vehicles, buses, taxis, cyclists and emergency and disabled persons' vehicles. Travel speeds on the light rail would be comparable, if not better, than travel over similar distances on the tube, where time is lost to reach the platforms. This would also help reduce congestion on the tube where it is used for short-distance travel. The Circle Line, however, would be upgraded, to improve its frequency, with lifts installed at every station to give easy access to platforms. This would be of particular benefit to tourists, because it is such an easily comprehensible and useful system for them within the centre.

These changes would require considerable political will to bring about. However a phased approach, making immediate improvements to public transport, for example, to the bus system, or to improve cycling conditions are possible

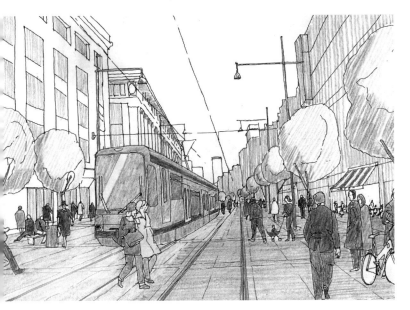

6.34
Car-free London Competition, 1999 (see p. 73). An ideas competition organised by the Architecture Foundation. A highly commended entry by the author. View along a car-free Oxford Street with two-way light rail to take the place of buses. Extensive tree planting and a repaved street, eliminating kerbs, with numerous outdoor cafes.

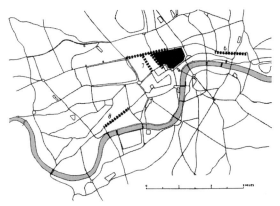

6.35
Years 1 and 2. Phased pedestrian improvements to centre. Some of these, together with the first phase of the light rail system, would start before road pricing was introduced. Starts with Saturday-only trial street closures to all traffic on shopping streets.

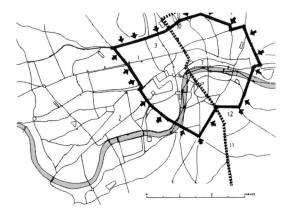

6.36
Year 3. Construction of north–south light rail system followed by the start of the road pricing cordon. Free shoppers' buses introduced within the cordon area.

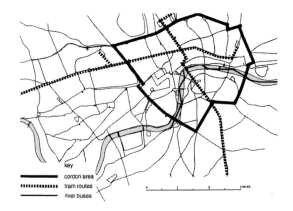

6.37
Year 8. East–west light rail opened – possibly extended later to Paddington and to Shepherd's Bush to reduce the need for building Crossrail.

6.38

Typical detail around a street junction: a pedestrian-only Oxford Street with two-way light rail running at frequent intervals; the adjacent existing multi-storeyed car park would be for the use of residents, car clubs and cycle hire; free shoppers' buses would serve the side streets; short-term electric cars which are shown on the left together with taxi stands; most roads crossing Oxford Street would be closed to traffic to reduce delays to the light rail system.

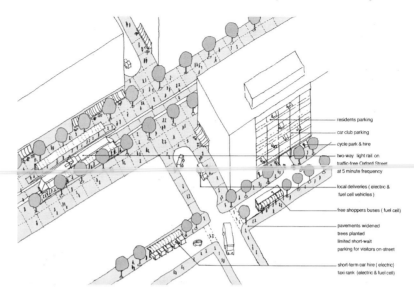

residents parking
car club parking
cycle park & hire
two-way light rail on traffic-free Oxford Street at 5 minute frequency
local deliveries (electric & fuel cell vehicles)
free shoppers buses (fuel cell)
pavements widened
trees planted
limited short-wait parking for visitors on-street
short-term car hire (electric) taxi rank (electric & fuel cell)

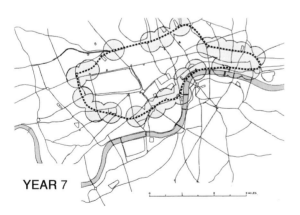

YEAR 7

6.39

Underground. The Circle Line, widely used by tourists as an easily comprehensible and useful system in the centre, would be upgraded to give a three-minute frequency. Lift access from ground level would be provided to all platforms (easier because the line is shallow). Stations would be refurbished, with improved safe access on foot provided at ground level within a five-minute walking distance of each station (shown ringed).

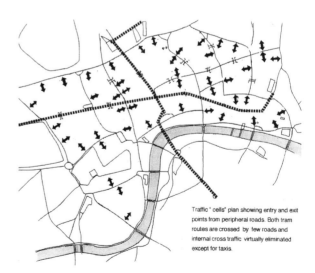

Traffic " cells" plan showing entry and exit points from peripheral roads. Both tram routes are crossed by few roads and internal cross traffic virtually eliminated except for taxis.

6.40

Servicing. Diagram showing entry/exit points off perimeter ring road for delivery vans and for public access to hotels. Shows limited crossing of light rail routes except by shoppers' buses, emergency vehicles and cyclists.

and should help. It would need to be implemented by a highly motivated team of traffic engineers, planners, landscape architects. A press office whose sole role would be to continually keep the public informed and enthusiastic about progress would be essential. Other cities have done this successfully, some spurred on by the imminent arrival of the Olympics as well as having a powerful Mayor. It happened in Munich, and later in Barcelona, with both cities transformed as a result. The Sydney Olympics should also be mentioned. This proved to be a great success, and was a unique experiment in showing how such an event, which allowed for very limited access by private car, in an intensely car-oriented city, could attract people into using public transport due to the quality of the systems provided.

This chapter suggests how public transport and vehicles might be handled in any future city adopting road pricing. It applies principally to those cities whose centre is too large to walk across, larger than from one or two kilometres across, where road space is limited. Many historic towns and cities in Europe with centres of this size and inner ring roads around them are already virtually car-free, simply by moving parking to the periphery with some providing for movement across the centre by light rail. London is, of course, a special case, with a large central area, but with narrow roads making efficient, surface-level public transport difficult to run, unless cars are firmly controlled. Paris, in direct contrast, has wide boulevards and buses can easily be given bus-only lanes. In practice these are frequently disregarded and parking controls are notoriously lax. The end result is that many fine areas of the city are destroyed environmentally.

In spite of the title of the competition, the solutions discussed above did not arrive at a car-free proposal. That seemed to be too simplistic a solution. Perhaps in 25 years' time it will be more generally accepted as being possible. What it aimed to show was how, in many areas of the larger cities, zones could be created where streets can be a pleasure to walk on and safe to cycle with attractive public transport readily available. If this, at least, was achieved, it would help make the city a better and more enjoyable place in which to live and work.

Chapter 7

Future sub-centres

Sub-centres occur normally outside city centres, providing offices to serve a daytime population of professional people, or businesses, who do not need to be in the city centre. Sub-centres rely on good connections by public transport and road, both with the city centre and with other sub-centres. They have the potential for imaginative planning and design, with none of the restraints associated with developing within the historic core areas. Many now provide shops, restaurants, hotels and residential accommodation.

Examples of two sub-centres are briefly discussed, both containing many of the elements to be found in any future centres: La Défense, in Paris, a megastructure development now virtually complete after 35 years; and Canary Wharf in London's Docklands, which began in 1985 and is continuing construction. Both have one thing in common. Although providing for car access with a high parking content they rely on access by public transport. Unlike the Edge Cities built in the United States they have been built compactly, attempting to avoid the environmental problems associated with planning for car access in the cheapest possible way.

La Défense, Paris

This is one of nine sub-centres or new towns planned around Paris in the 1950s to take the pressure off the historic core. Built on the west side of Paris, on the axis of the Champs Elysées, La Défense has today 140,000 people working in offices, many of them in tower blocks, situated along an elevated deck around 100 m wide

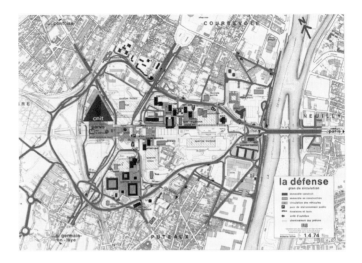

7.2
Road plan showing one-way peripheral motorway from which access roads lead to parking at intervals for 36,000 cars situated below deck level.

7.1
La Défense, Paris. View looking west along central deck. High-rise buildings on either side are offices for 100,000 with some apartments.

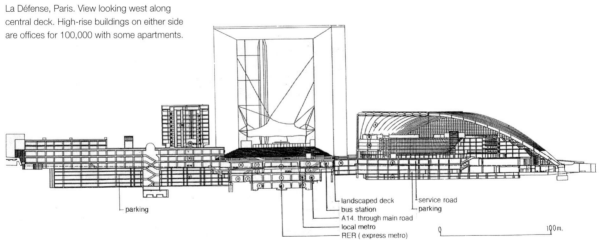

landscaped deck
bus station
A14. through main road
local metro
RER (express metro)
service road
parking
parking

0   100 m.

7.3
North–south section through the central deck raised to around four storeys above the surrounding streets. The main through road, the A14, is shown below the deck with the local metro with two stations alongside, serving the deck, an extension of the old Paris metro. At the lowest level is the RER, the express metro, with one station at the west end of the deck. Parking for 36,000 cars is located on either side of the deck, served by the peripheral motorway at the outer edges. Courtesy: EPAD.

and 1.2 km long. A one-way peripheral motorway encircles the development, enclosing an area of 170 hectare and gives access to 12 multi-level parking silos for 36,000 cars. All parking has to be paid for and no on-street parking is allowed.

The central deck, beautifully planted by the American landscape architect Dan Kiley, has avenues of trees and covered walkways to help protect pedestrians from the winds caused by the high buildings. Below the deck (see Figure 7.3) at the lowest level is the RER (Regional Express metro) which reaches the centre of Paris in 15 minutes and extends east to Nanterre, where a new university is located, and is capable of carrying up to 60,000 passengers an hour with one station serving La Défense. Above this is the through road, the A14, formerly planned as a motorway, now reduced to two one-way roads in order to allow for a metro line, recently constructed, with two stations serving the deck and connecting with the main city metro system. At the west end of the deck the principle bus station is located with bus links to the neighbouring suburbs. Also at this end of the deck below the building known as the Grand Arche is the main line station. Around 75 per cent of workers and visitors arrive by any one of these four modes of public transport and there is a resident population of 20,000 people living in 9,000 flats, served by a large hypermarket, with numerous shops and cafes situated along the length of the deck.

The construction of La Défense, like many similar schemes, including Canary Wharf, has gone through difficult times during the recession in the 1970s. One serious problem concerning the phased construction was having a deck only built in stages, situated three storeys above ground level and how to gain access to office blocks which had their entrance halls three storeys above ground. These had to be served by temporary bridges until the deck was complete.

The design of the peripheral motorway system (see Figure 7.2) with its free-flowing intersections, is problematic for drivers and reflects the thinking of the period. Traffic engineers, largely influenced by American examples, were then oblivious to the eventual problems of traffic congestion, or the need, to design a road system which could be sympathetic to the 'grain' of the neighbouring areas as well as not present a barrier, which this one does. The roads, designed for fast traffic, in practice make it hard for a driver to identify appropriate entry points to parking serving the office towers and which, once missed, requires a complete circumferential tour for a second try. Similarly at EuroLille (see Figure 2.15) the geometry of the road system has the same faults, although those roads adjacent to the new station were simplified. For all its faults and its forbidding architecture, La Défense still represents an interesting and ambitious attempt to integrate public transport into a large-scale complex.

Canary Wharf, London

Canary Wharf is part of an area formerly occupied by docks. Building started in 1980 and at present consists of 13 office blocks with 9 million sq ft. Within this are retail stores, restaurants and a conference centre. By 2002 Canary Wharf will house a population of around 50,000 people, expected to reach 100,000 when completed. Part of the development consists of 300 apartments and a 140-room hotel is under construction nearby with extensive housing within walking distance.

The scheme is served by a heavily congested road system and provides parking for 3,000 cars underground. Because of traffic congestion, around 50 per cent of drivers arrive before 8am and around 60 per cent leave after 6pm with only 15 per cent of employees driving. The parking is situated below an elevated deck, unlike La Défense, only one level above the surrounding ground level, with easy connections on foot to the surrounding areas, by stairs and lifts. This deck has a one-way road running around on it, carrying buses and taxis, which has to be crossed by pedestrians. Public transport to Canary Wharf is by seven bus services linking with the local areas. The Docklands Light Railway (DLR), a driverless system with an elevated station in the centre of the development, provides access to the City of London, the main financial centre, in ten minutes with a three-minute frequency at peak periods. Finally the new Jubilee Line extension, part of the London Underground, has a station adjacent, designed to handle 20,000 passengers an hour although remote, as the plan shows, from the DLR station. Like La Défense, the public transport links are a vital part of Canary Wharf's success and an estimated 84 per cent of employees in the development use public transport, or walk.

The planning and design of these two sub-centres, together with their transport infrastructure, are indicative of planning theory of around 25 years ago when little thought was given to the importance of providing decent spaces for the pedestrian. Both schemes have a high office content and are largely dead at night and at weekends. By day the environment for pedestrians differs. La Défense, with an overscaled central deck, offers little delight in spite of fine landscaping, with windswept spaces without animation. Canary Wharf offers even less, with one small town square and fountain and an enclosed shopping mall which gives no direct access to the offices above.

Future residential areas

Future residential areas will be served by a variety of transport systems from private cars, buses, cycles and mopeds to more innovatory systems, from electric

7.5
View of DLR station at Canary Wharf. The high-level outer platforms connect directly into shopping on either side. This line gives access into the City, London's business centre, in 15 minutes and carries up to 16,000 passengers an hour in one direction.

7.4
Canary Wharf, London's Docklands. High-level view looking south showing elevated DLR station situated between two office blocks. The area in the foreground currently used for car parking is under development. Photo: Chorley & Hanford.

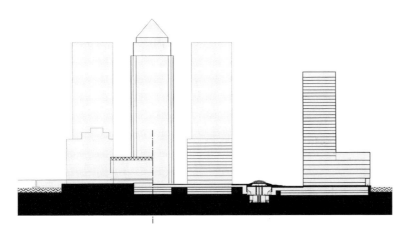

7.6
North–south cross section looking east showing the relation of the deck, with the ground level terraces bordering the docks. Shopping is situated below deck with two levels below for parking 3,000 cars used by an esitmated 15 per cent of the working population, with the rest arriving by public transport or on foot.

7.7
View looking south across Heron Quays from Canary Wharf to DLR elevated tracks.

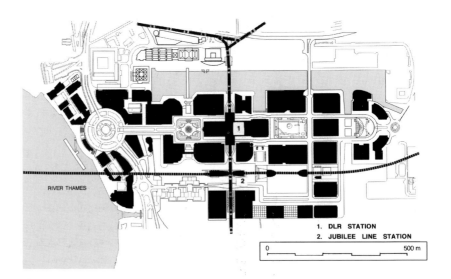

1. DLR STATION
2. JUBILEE LINE STATION

7.8
Site plan of Canary Wharf development to be shortly completed. The north–south line is the route of the elevated light railway (DLR) with a central station (1). The east–west line is the route of the Jubilee Line with a single station serving it (2). Interchange between the two is remote.

cars (see p. 114) to personal rapid transit. More people will be working from home due to the growth of computer technology which will, for some, reduce the need to travel to work each day. Tele-shopping will allow householders or office workers to order their weekly shopping on the screen, for deliveries to be made to their homes, or to select their home-video, to be beamed to their screens, without the need to visit the shop. Online systems will, in theory, reduce the need for people to leave home, but in practice it is unlikely to eliminate travel. People will want to get out and face-to-face contact will remain important (Mitchell, 2000). Downtown areas or local sub-centres, too, will provide cultural or sports activities, which people will want to enjoy and to meet other people.

In areas of 'old-style' suburban living with high car ownership, few changes in travel patterns are likely to occur and houses, at a low density, with provision for two cars per household, are likely to continue to be built as long as there is the demand, they are saleable and land can be found. Only where a combination of soaring land costs, high petrol prices, combined with gridlock on the roads occurs, will there be any changes likely to happen. In some countries, planning intervention could change the present pattern of development at low densities more rapidly given the political will. A total ban on encroachment into green belt land, for example, could encourage planning at higher densities in the suburbs, as well as building on brownfield land within the cities.

There will be opportunities for new dense housing development to occur in areas such as on redundant railway land. In order to be successful, good public transport has to be provided. It is essential to build housing with good systems of public transport available. Light rail stops or metro stations, for example, could form the local node points for any neighbourhood. At these points, ideally, local shops, offices and community facilities would be located within easy walking distance, or cycle ride, from each home. Montpellier's new light rail already has provisional sites for two additional stops, to serve housing schemes being completed.

The low-density dilemma

Housing densities in the US at 12 persons/hectare are normal. Although average UK densities are around double this, they are still half that found in the rest of Europe. In the US, with high car ownership, cheap petrol and in most cases free parking, there is little incentive within residential areas to run more than a skeleton bus service, although in some residential areas of cities, often where car ownership is low, small bus fleets run successfully. In the case of the UK, where a combination of road tax, high petrol costs and parking charges exists, a minimum subsidised bus service will be normally run, essential for the carless, but rarely

7.9
Hoppa buses with a capacity of around 50 people, with wheelchair access, used in lower residential areas in London.

7.10
Jeepneys in Manila. Brightly painted fleet of over 36,000 vehicles which stop on demand and carry around 14 people. Popular and cheap to use and widely used in developing countries.

providing a service good enough to attract car owners on to it. Dial a ride services, heavily subsidised, provided by the local authority use minibuses equipped with boarding platforms to serve older or disabled people. These are only on an occasional basis, not for daily trips to work. Recent experiments using minibuses, costing around £250 a day to run, in Hackney, London, have shown that this is a preferred system, running on a fixed route at half hourly intervals, to dial a ride, which is door to door.

In many areas taxis play an important role, particularly in more affluent areas and may also be used by old people, who do not own cars, or do not want to drive, or to ferry children to school because walking or cycling is considered too dangerous. Taxis in the future will remain an important system of transport. In Holland and Germany they provide late-night transport from rail and light rail stations, on demand. In developing countries where labour is cheap and insurance laws are disregarded, taxis of varying sizes, from three wheeled tuk-tuks to minibuses, form the principal systems of public transport. In the residential areas of many cities in developing countries, such as Mexico City, taxis and minibuses ferry people to and from home, run either along fixed routes or from homes to the nearest rail or metro station. These often provide the convenience of door-to-door service, at low cost, which no conventional public transport system can offer. Only as the numbers increase, in the more congested areas of the city, do they become self-defeating (Cervero, 1998).

Future suburbs planned at a density of 100 persons/hectare would allow around 5,000 people to be only 600 m walk from local centres (UTF). These centres would provide shops and ideally employment, with small offices or light industry. Local roads would be traffic calmed with cycle lanes and minibuses, or subsidised taxis used to serve areas too far to walk and also act as feeder systems to the nearest express bus or light rail stop. Improved walking or cycling conditions would be ideally along roads designed for slow-moving traffic (30 kph; 20 mph), now being implemented in some German residential areas. Previously roads and their junctions were designed for higher speeds in direct conflict with pedestrian safety.

Car clubs or car sharing clubs, already widely used in Europe, are starting in the UK and North America. They have been found to reduce car ownership and use by as much as 50 per cent (see p. 102) although this depends on the availability and quality of public transport. StattAuto in Germany with over 20,000 members in 18 cities, offers a range of vehicle sizes to members, according to need. In the future club members will be able to use club cars in different ways, equipped with 'smart technology' which automatically identifies each vehicle at a central control room, allowing it to be booked as required. For example a permanently rented car, which might be electric, is kept at home, used for the daily drive to a local transit station, possibly shared with other commuters. It is then parked, for use by other members during the day who have booked its use, returning it on time to the station for the commuters' return trip (Shaheen *et al.*, 1999).

Intelligent cars and highways

Some cross-town trips might involve driving, so new 'intelligent' computer technology will inform our thrice-weekly commuter about travel conditions. Before leaving home our commuter will consult the travel section on his or her screen, flagging up a choice of travel modes, with likely travel times for each. Having selected to drive, possibly because of the complexity of the trip, our driver, collecting a car from the local club parking place, will feed in the required destination, be told if a congestion-free route is possible, where and if parking was available and reserve this prior to arrival. The trip may not involve a visit to an office. Office work will increasingly involve hot-desking, with the possibility of working more within the car and our driver's own mobile phone can send and receive e-mail. The drive on the motorway may even involve meeting clients at a new motorway 'workplace', already being built in the UK by Granada, attached to a drive-in service station, where facilities for video conferencing, and secretarial services are available for a fee.

It might be possible that, as the main roads reach saturation point, a new kind of vehicle is necessary, one with the characteristics of a private car, non-polluting and automated for the longer distances. In this case a small contract-hired electric car could be used, such as the Alden StarrCar (see pp. 42 and 125), normally a hire car, possibly garaged at home or picked up locally, and driven on the local roads to a local entry-point adjacent to the freeway. Here the required destination would be booked and, once the vehicle is checked, it will drive itself under electric power on the automated section beside the freeway, until the appropriate exit point is reached. The car would then be driven to its required destination on the normal road system, to be used for the return trip.

This technology has been tried (see above, Chapter 4, 'Automated highways'); but the question remains of when such a scenario will, if ever, take place and where. Traffic congestion, for example, in parts of California have now reached such a level, where freeway building has stopped, that a system of this kind, in some areas like Silicon Valley, might already be economic and be less costly or space-consuming than building more freeways. Such a system would have the advantages of producing virtually zero pollution and take up around one-third the amount of parking space required at any workplace.

In direct contrast to using advanced automotive technology of this kind, the alternative is to make public transport so attractive that more people will forego

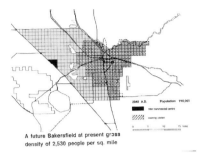

A future Bakersfield at present gross
density of 2,530 people per sq. mile

7.11

Growth of Bakersfield, to 900,000 people,
assuming the present density continues at
2,530 people per sq mile. Showing a scenario
with an 'edge city' development on the west
side adjacent to Route 5, the north–south
freeway and the dissolution of the present
downtown.

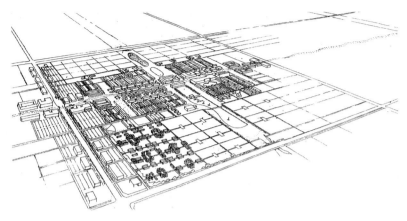

7.12

Great Central Valley Competition. Bakersfield, Southern California. Sketch of a typical square mile
block to house 10,000 people at around twice the present density.

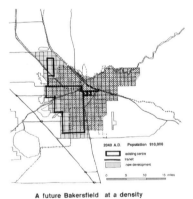

A future Bakersfield at a density
of 10,000 people per sq. mile

7.13

Growth based on one mile square
development, to 900,000 people by 2040 at a
density of 10,000 people per sq mile. Good
bus links maintained with the present city
centre which would be revitalised.

7.14

Sketch of central mall for buses, taxis and cycles. Three-storeyed family apartments showing
ground floor arcades with some shops, small offices and workplaces.

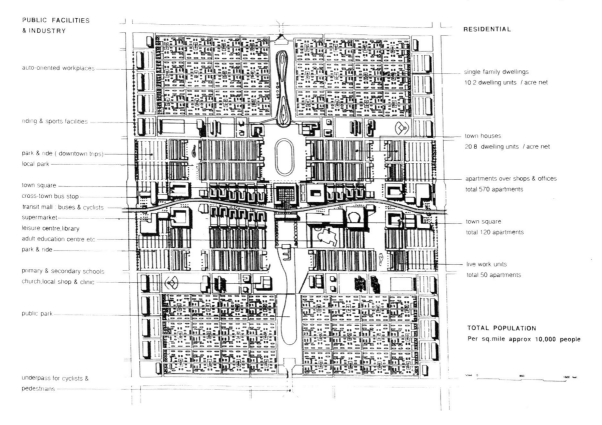

PUBLIC FACILITIES
& INDUSTRY

auto-oriented workplaces

riding & sports facilities

park & ride (downtown trips)
local park

town square
cross-town bus stop
transit mall : buses & cyclists
supermarket
leisure centre, library
adult education centre etc
park & ride

primary & secondary schools
church, local shop & clinic

public park

underpass for cyclists &
pedestrians

RESIDENTIAL

single family dwellings
10.2 dwelling units / acre net

town houses
20.8 dwelling units / acre net

apartments over shops & offices
total 570 apartments

town square
total 120 apartments

live work units
total 50 apartments

TOTAL POPULATION
Per sq.mile approx 10,000 people

7.15

Plan of typical mile square block housing 10,000 people – around twice the present density. Shows a central bus mall that links each block together and with the existing city centre.

7.16

Detail of section of bus mall. Four-storeyed apartments with ground-level shops and small offices and workshops line the mall, intended as a promenade area in the evenings to be enjoyed by the high proportion of Mexican immigrant population. The busway would be used by buses, cycles and taxis. Project by West and Richards, Architects with Curzon-Price.

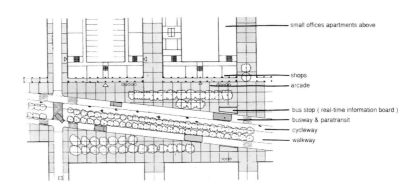

small offices apartments above

shops
arcade

bus stop (real-time information board)
busway & paratransit
cycleway
walkway

using their cars, at least for commuting. One approach would be to build new communities around low-key transport. This is shown in a commended competition entry, submitted in 1998, by the author and George West, as architects, with Curzon Price, a philosopher, for a city in the Great Central Valley in California. This ideas competition, organised by the American Institute of Architects, aimed at showing to the communities in the Valley alternative ways of dealing with a projected increase in population of 20 million people in the next 20 years (see pp. 86, 87).

The proposal shows how Bakersfield, in Southern California, could be increased by 500,000 people by constructing in stages a series of 1 mile square communities or townships, each containing around 10,000 people. Housed at varying densities – at an average of 38 persons/hectare, double the local density – a mixture of individual homes, terraced town houses, would be built with four-storeyed, low-cost family apartments. These would be built adjacent to a bus-only pedestrian mall, along which would run buses and taxis with cyclists. Small shops, workshops, with offices would be situated at ground level, below the apartments, aimed at generating pedestrian activity. The high number of Mexican residents living in the area, with their tradition of promenading in the evenings, would help keep the mall lively. Buses and shared taxis would circulate between each community and along the mall, connecting into the existing downtown area.

Each township would have local workspaces, live-work units, and so reduce the necessity of driving to work. Streets would be traffic-calmed, so that walking a distance of up to four minutes on tree-lined pavements, or two minutes on a cycle, to shop would be accepted in an area where today almost no one is seen on the sidewalks, fairly typical in this part of California.

Transport in the suburbs

So are there any other solutions to the transport problems associated with living in the car-oriented suburb of tomorrow and why bother to change it? Clearly 'there is a deeply felt gut feeling [in the United States] that . . . the heavily auto-dependent society lacks something' (Cervero, 1998). There may even be a move there towards going back to live in city centres again in the US, or at least try to revitalise their centres for leisure use. But what to do about it? One is to do nothing, except as has been suggested wait until land values and other factors lead to a change of thinking, finally finding its way into the minds of the house-building entrepreneurs and a population wanting a new lifestyle. The solution of attempting to restructure suburbs around a popular system of public transport, as Portland is attempting, is interesting. Light rail is already being tried in many cities in the US largely closely tied to park and ride as a way of reducing the pressure on road

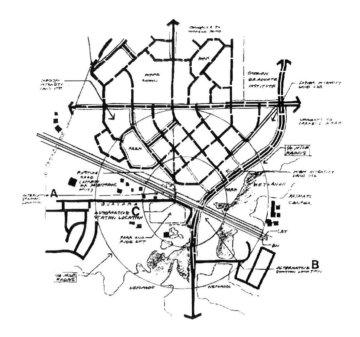

7.17

Portland, Oregon. An example of a four-storeyed housing layout around a light rail station, planned at Hillsboro on the Westside Max line, intended to improve the walking catchment within a 400 m radius. Courtesy: Tri-Met.

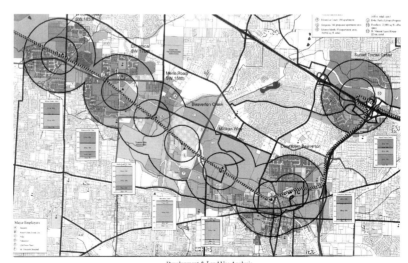

Development & Land Use Analysis
Westside MAX Station Areas
Beaverton, Oregon
April 1997

7.18

Land-use development plan on section of Westside Max line running through existing neighbourhoods. Since completion, this has encouraged $500 million of new development, together with 7,000 new homes, all within walking distance of stops. Courtesy: Tri-Met.

space. In Europe it is proving to attract people out of their cars and help reinforce in many cases the role of downtown areas. New systems, relatively untried, like personal rapid transit (see PRT, Chapter 3) may in the future provide a flexibility of movement which light rail does not.

In Portland, Oregon, on its new Westside Max line, which connects to the city centre, unbuilt land along the route is being developed, with transit villages of housing, shops and some offices at the stations at higher densities – some of which have been laid out with streets radiating from several stations. Buses feed into stations and serve areas beyond walking distance. Portland's light rail provides fast travel to its centre with 95 per cent of passengers car owners. Here it has encouraged business to locate with no increased parking provision. It has attracted new development, such as industry along its routes, where developers see apparent advantages of only five minutes' walk from stations.

This is a success story that deserves special mention. Having still an essentially car-based population, Portland's citizens make only 61 trips in any one year on public transport (compared to Zurich's 800). However in North American terms this remains an important and unique experiment, a lesson there for future city growth. Because it has adopted a planned approach to integrated transport, Portland has nurtured an image of sustainability and good sense and has been successful in bringing business to the city, as well as improving the quality of life of its inhabitants.

Low density and long walks

How to deal with short trips of 2–4 km from homes remains, as ever, one of the major problems of transport in any residential area. So far not enough examples of planned communities designed by the group known as the New Urbanists, have been realised on the West Coast of the US, to show that the densities proposed or the street designs will really encourage walking. Neither will the transit (meaning trams) shown in the layouts materialise, if there is not the demand for them. Buses, apart from the excellent electric fleet in the centre of Santa Barbara, are not very well used in affluent suburbs. Why walk, or wait for a bus if you can drive, as long as you can afford a car, petrol is cheap and parking is free? Light rail, or commuter rail is more popular, serving downtown areas, is well used in many cities in the US, with stations providing parking, but rarely providing for attractive access on foot.

In Europe this stage has not quite been reached, although it could happen as car ownership increases. There are already intensely car-oriented communities in every country. London statistics (Public transport in London, Market Report 2000) show that car-owning households make five times as many car trips as the bus trips made in non-car-owning households. However it has been shown that once rail or metro is available their use is less affected by car ownership. Zurich, Switzerland has the most widely used public transport system in Europe and a population making 800 trips a year, yet it barely keeps passengers on its system in spite of having severe car restraint on parking in its central areas.

Cycling

Cycling will suit a proportion of people. With properly planned cycle lanes for them to use, or safe streets with slow-moving traffic to ride on, if these measures are taken in countries which do not already have them, they will help make cycling more popular. At present, while there are more cycles owned in the UK than cars,

7.19
More cycles are now sold annually in Europe than cars. All that is required are more routes like this one in Amsterdam, Holland, which can be used safely. Photo: Stef Breukel, Klats Publiciteit, Delft.

7.20
Motorised scooter sales doubled in London in one year and are now likely to increase in the future as long as people continue to be frustrated with public transport.

only 2 per cent of journeys are made by cycle compared to Denmark's 18 per cent. Increased traffic on the roads has contributed to this, and the figure is expected to improve as new measures to improve cycling conditions are introduced. Providing secure cycle parking has to be an essential part of any cycling 'package' at transit stations, shops or offices. This is an economic use of space, taking up one-tenth of ground space compared to cars (100 cycles in the space of 10 cars). Dutch railway stations, for example, have 97,000 guarded depots for cycles, with 67,000 unguarded cycle stands and 35 per cent of rail passengers cycle to stations.

In Japan, cycling to stations is so popular and takes up so much space that multi-level parking is often built. In newly planned areas, sufficient space for cycle lanes can be provided beside roads, at the planning stage, as well as parking space. Proper provision for secure cycle parking has to be an essential requirement for residents, within higher density development. Cycle storage lockers or secure storage areas have to be provided at ground level and secure parking racks for visitors' cycles. The Edinburgh car-free scheme (see p. 99) is an example of this with secure rooms for cycles at ground level beside the entrance to every access stair. One solution to cycle security, which is currently being tried out, is an essential part of a hire system, now operating in Rennes, France, and Singapore. Here club members are given free 'smart cards' which, when inserted into a box beside the cycle, securely fastened in a rack at a 'docking station', releases it for short-term use. The cycle can be used, for up to two hours and returned to any of the other 'stations' for use by others (see p. 120).

Mention should be made of motorised cycles, which can involve anything from motorbikes, licensed as cars, to scooters and electric cycles. In Italy, the use of scooters, such as the Vespa, has reached epidemic proportion. These require parking space and are frequently allowed into controlled areas. Florence, for example, experienced severe problems over pollution from scooters although with new cleaner engines these are becoming increasingly popular. Electric bikes, which are silent and non-polluting, are used by a number of police forces in the United States. As to which, if any, of these vehicles should be allowed to use cycle lanes, is debatable.

High- and low-density living

With housing built at higher densities, dealing with car parking is an important factor. The aim of providing for as much green space as possible at ground level means that car parking has either to be located under the buildings, at ground level which is problematic visually, or underground, with parkland on top. Ralph

Erskine's prizewinning scheme for Millennium Village, in Greenwich, London, provides parking within earth berms at ground level, with turf above, at the periphery of some of the housing. In Skarpnack (pp. 94, 95), Stockholm, the solution is to provide parking for the 28 per cent of families who own cars, in a number of multi-storeyed silos, to allow a more compact overall plan. Parking underground is more expensive, around ten times that of surface parking, but the environmental advantages are considerable. Once residents are separated from their cars, which in low-density housing are parked outside their front doors or in their own garages, there may be more incentive to walk or cycle for local trips, particularly if they are conducted through a civilised, traffic-free environment.

In Singapore the government strategy is to make cars so expensive that under 50 per cent of residents have them and good public transport is essential. But this

7.21

Greenwich, London. The Millennium Village first phase contains 140 homes built at a density of 80 dwellings/ha to a master plan by Ralph Erskine. The bus-only road and cycleway (3) links to the North Greenwich underground station. Low-rise housing along the dual carriageway is approached by pedestrian-only roads with car parking (5), situated in landscaped areas at the periphery. The high-rise housing fronting the River Thames (7) has parking below. Courtesy: Greenwich Millennium Village.

0   100 m

1. Residential area
2. Bus stop
3. Bus-only road &
   cycleway
4. Pedestrian-only streets
5. Car parking
6. To North Greenwich underground
   station 5 minutes walk
7. River Thames

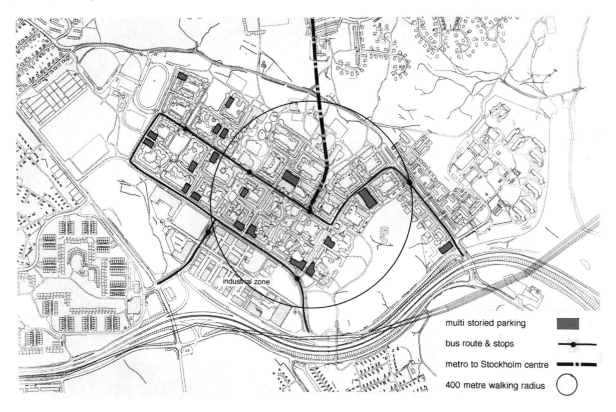

7.22

Stockholm, Sweden. Plan of Skarpnack, a neighbourhood for 10,000 people in South Stockholm. This is laid out on a gridiron pattern of high-rise flats with central gardens at a density of 120 dwellings/ha. A single bus route crosses the centre and a large proportion of the housing is within 400 m walk of the underground station (shown) which links to Central Stockholm. Car parking is within multi-storeyed towers serving around 50 per cent of families who own cars.

is an exceptional case and does not seem to reduce a desire for people to have cars or to drive. In one high-rise scheme, the local car club was swamped with applications for membership. In the dense housing scheme illustrated (see Figure 7.27) at Sengkiang, a satellite new town for 150,000 people, an elevated automatic transit system runs in two loops through the scheme with stations 200–300 m from each building, often integrated into local centres. This gives easy access to shops and links with the central interchange station with a direct connection to the metro, underground metro running to the downtown area. The pictures still show parking between the buildings at ground level.

More promising are the new Japanese residential towns being built outside

7.23
View of tree-lined shopping street opposite the metro station and within walking distance of all homes, with minimal street parking and served by small buses.

7.24
View along main shopping street and bus route adjacent to underground station.

7.25
High-level view showing internal courtyard system, each containing gardens for ground-level flats. All residents' car parking is situated in separate parking towers. Courtesy: Stockholm Stadsbyggnadskontor.

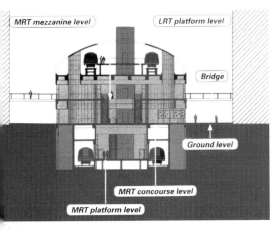

7.26
Section through central station with LRT at high level and MRT at subway level linking to the centre of Singapore. Courtesy: Urban Redevelopment Authority, Singapore.

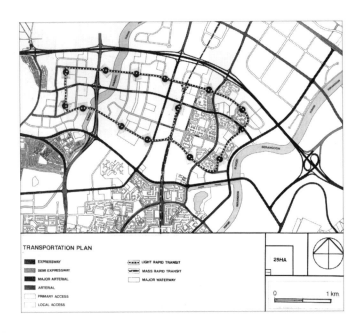

7.27
Sengkiang, Singapore. The first new town, housing 150,000 people, to include, at the planning stage, a fixed automatic transit system (LRT). The plan shows the catchment of 300 m around the stations of the figure-of-eight loop which crosses to interchange with the underground in the middle.

7.28
View of typical elevated LRT system used at a similar neighbourhood at Punggol. Courtesy: Adtranz.

Tokyo, laid out around new subway lines. Here shops and offices are located around each station with low-rise housing and segregated pathway systems, radiating from the station, for walking and cycling to the stations (see Figures 7.29, 7.30).

Finally there is the alternative approach of making the housing part of a car-free area, served by good public transport. This might involve the formation of a local car club, as has occurred in the Edinburgh scheme (see p. 99). Within dense areas of a city this could be the way forward with the acceptance of policies to eliminate the present car parking required by local authorities which can be as much as two car spaces per dwelling. Once car clubs were seen to be popular, developers of housing schemes would be more interested in providing them as part of the overall project, which would help reduce the amount of parking. A long-term view suggested (Shaheen *et al.*, 1999) would be the formation of mobility companies who would provide a 'package' to householders on an estate, handling the insurance, maintenance and registration of vehicles, providing one as and when required, together with dealing with the local transit system.

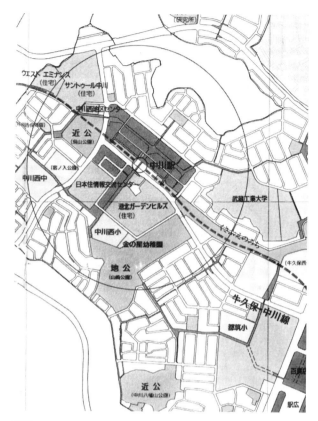

7.30
View of a typical community street combining pedestrians and cyclists, with play areas for children in Toyou Kotou-Ku New Town, Japan. Photo: Yoshio Tsukio.

7.29
Khoku New Town, outside Tokyo. Housing 160,000 people and connected by subway. This station at Nakagawa is one of six underground stations serving the town. The layout around the station on one side of the underground tracks is for business use, with dense housing on the other. Car-free pedestrian streets, called community streets, run from the station entrance connecting with the surrounding residential areas. Courtesy: Urban Development Corporation.

Car-free housing

This is a relatively new phenomenon which has grown as an idea across Europe as a result of the popular demand from residents for safer streets and less street parking. Town yards, called *woonerven*, started in Delft in the 1970s and now numbering over 6,500, provide safe play-streets for children and the landscaping of streets with the removal of the footpath. This was only possible in areas where few residents owned cars and streets were narrow. As car ownership increases so streets become impossible to landscape in the same way and it is perhaps because of community action that there are areas where this approach is changing.

Car-free housing, as a concept, has obvious advantages for the people living in the surrounding areas. Streets without cars are safe, quiet and cleaner, with more public space available for landscaping. The car-free Edinburgh housing scheme, discussed below, has its central courtyard, but rather than being filled with cars, which occurs in so many low-cost housing schemes, this is landscaped with safer areas for children to play, private gardens for ground level flats and ponds and reed beds to clean waste water.

The Borough of Camden, in London, has now relaxed previous parking requirements for housing in the central areas, with 58 schemes passed by the Council. The trade-off for developers is obvious. More space is available for gardens and landscaping, and apartments can be made larger through providing no off-street parking spaces. Residents, however, are not allowed to apply for street parking permits but cannot legally be stopped from owning cars, using private car parks, or joining a car club.

The availability of public transport is one important factor in making car-free housing acceptable, as well as the availability of car clubs. In Zurich, for example, with the highest daily usage of public transport in Europe, one-third of households do not own cars (388 cars per 1,000 households) and 9,000 residents in Greater Zurich are members of a car club (Cervero, 1998). In London single cars are owned by around 50 per cent of households.

A scheme built for the Canmore Housing Association in Edinburgh for 120 flats is situated adjacent to two main roads with 5–6 bus services going into the centre on each road, and the city only a 15 minute walk away. Here only 30 per cent of tenants owned cars and while the scheme does not allow them to bring them on to the site, they all sign legal agreements which allows them to own cars but keep them elsewhere, or alternatively they can join the local car club. A small parking area is provided for visitor parking.

In Amsterdam, in the Westerpark district, a partly car-free housing project has been built with 600 dwelling units in an area of 6 hectares. Car parking is limited to 100 spaces, assigned to residents by lottery, with 25 spaces for visitors. An estimated 110 residents gave up their cars when they moved in (Beatley 2000). Shops, a community centre, schools and a day-care centre are within walking

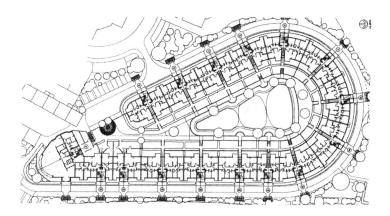

7.31 *above*
Edinburgh, Scotland. Car-free housing scheme for Canmore Housing Association. View of the internal courtyard, a space frequently used in similar layouts for car parking, used here as children's play space, with gardens and pools for recirculating waste water. Architects: Hackland & Dore.

7.32 *above and top*
Edinburgh. Plan views of car-free housing, comprising 120 flats built around a private courtyard. Residents cannot bring cars on to the site but can join the local car club. Two bus routes to the city centre run close by and secure parking rooms are provided for cycles at each staircase. Architects: Hackland & Dore.

distance and there is a car club on the site. The space saved by reducing the area for parking has been assigned to garden plots and vegetable gardens. This highly successful experiment could well be the first of many such projects.

The examples discussed show some of the possiblities for building housing without the off-street space currently required by so many local authorities and which disregards the fact that the occupants might be without cars, either choosing not to have them for economic reasons or because they were elderly. In the Stockholm suburb of Skarpnack, for example (Figures 7.22–7.25), 50 per cent of residents, many of whom have retired, have no cars and do not need them because all the essential facilities, including work places, are within walking distance and good public transport is available. In the Amsterdam example, with an orientation towards 'eco development', the focus is on community gardens and space (which would otherwise be covered with cars), as well as a belief in a sustainable style of living. It is too early to say if car-free housing will become standard practice but there seems to be a strong case that it should be considered in new development areas where public transport is good.

Part III

The new transport technology

Chapter 8 New systems of transport

There is a wide range of systems of transport which are either in the process of being developed or have been over the last 30 years but are still relatively untried. In the nineteenth century inventors apparently had none of today's problems of liability or litigation. People wanted to embrace the new – that was the message. Systems such as the Paris moving pavement at the Great Exhibition of 1900, or the electric railway that ran beside it, used electric motors, newly arrived from America. Neither system had been tried before and yet were up and carrying people within two years (pp. 108, 109).

Today they would have had to conform to stringent guidelines laid down by official committees, often composed of manufacturers keen to keep the status quo as far as their companies products were concerned. Accidents today, even minor ones to individuals, can mean law suits and litigation. So today while safety is important, any move towards innovation in transport, however useful it might be, is not easy.

This chapter is about some of the more significant developments in city transport. They range from moving pavements to how small city cars are being used in different ways that could lead to a reduced demand for private ownership. Automated vehicles are shown, already commonplace in any airport and yet to be used seriously within cities. New kinds of bus are discussed together with new fuels which could transform their image. Finally, there is a section showing how surface-level transport is being successfully integrated into the streets of some European cities, freeing them of traffic.

8.1
Bilbao, Spain. View along the subway linking a station with the old town. Twin moving pavements with lighting within the handrails, together with an immaculate concrete lining to the tunnel with no advertising, add delight to the trip as you pop out into the historic town square at the end. Architects: Norman Foster and Partners.

8.2
New York, 1874. A proposal for an elevated moving sidewalk by Alfred Speer. The articulated
moving platforms ran along the inside on an elevated structure with waiting rooms at intervals.
Separate cabins, reached by stairs, accelerated to reach the same speed as the inner platform for
boarding. Source: *L'illustration, 1874.*

Moving pavements

The first proposals made for New York by Speer in 1874 showed that for them to
work over long distances they had to run either above or below streets and at reasonable speeds of 3 or 6 mph. Solutions then had to be found to the problem of how to
get on to or off them safely (Richards, 1966). It was then believed by their designers
that networks would run across a city centre in either direction. The first system was
built in 1983 for the World's Fair in Chicago. It ran at two speeds, in a loop on a pier
at the edge of Lake Michigan and was a great attraction. World fairs were seen to be
a fine opportunity for trying out new systems of transport – Osaka, Lausanne and
Montreal and recently Hanover are all examples of this and will be mentioned later.

The most notable system, built for the Paris Exhibition of 1900, ran in a one-
way, elevated loop around the edge of the grounds for a distance of 4 km and
carried six million fare-paying people in 8 months, paying for its cost with only six
accidents, none of which was serious. Here was a system which fired H.G. Wells
to write his classic book *When the Sleeper Awakes*, where a whole city would be
based on such a system of transport.

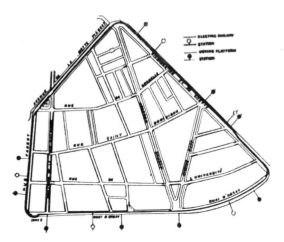

8.3
Paris Exhibition, 1900. Site plan of exhibition grounds, adjacent to the Eiffel Tower. Two systems of transport ran parallel with one another, elevated around the grounds. An electric railway on the inside with a moving pavement on the outside. Entry stairs to each system are indicated. Source: *Engineering*, London, 1900.

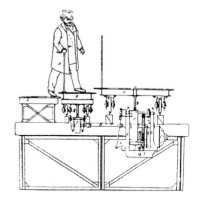

8.4
Section showing drive motors situated at intervals below the two outer platforms, both of which are driven from below by a continuous flexible rail, linking them together and driving them at speeds of 2 kph and 4 kph.

Since then moving pavements have been developed by escalator manufacturers, who have formulated codes of practice also applied to escalators, which travel at identical travel speeds of 2.4 km/hr, based on what is deemed a safe speed for boarding and leaving at either end. These run normally in lengths of around 100 m, end to end, with breaks of 10–15 m between each. They either use belts or platforms, like an escalator, and can move around 6,000 people an hour in one direction.

The most recent application of their use on a large scale was at the Osaka World Fair in 1970. Here 34 moving pavements, running elevated in air-conditioned, largely glazed tubes, were used as a structuring device for the whole exhibition. These were linked together to raised platforms, often forming the entry to a pavilion. Although heavily used, the slow travel speeds and the width of the belts did not allow people to pass one another, which made for tedious travel conditions. Today, manufacturers make wider systems, up to 1.4 m wide, which allow those walking to pass those standing.

8.5 *above and below*
Paris Exhibition. Two views of the 4 km long moving pavement system showing two-speed platforms with a fixed walkway on the right with access to ground-level ticket offices by stairs at intervals. The system carried over 6 million people in six months with few accidents and paid for the cost of construction. Source: Imprimerie Nationale, 1900.

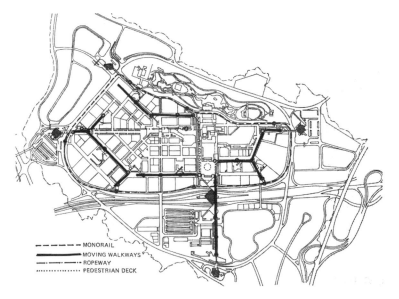

8.6
Osaka World's Fair, Japan, 1970. The layout plan, by Kenzo Tange, shows a monorail running around the periphery of the site connecting at pedestrian node points to the elevated moving pavement network. This ran within air-conditioned, semi-glazed tubes, between platforms often linked to the pavilions and was used as a structuring element in the plan.

8.7
View of elevated tube on left, containing moving pavements towards Kenzo Tange's Theme Pavilion. Courtesy: Koichi Sone, Architect.

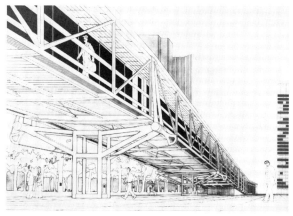

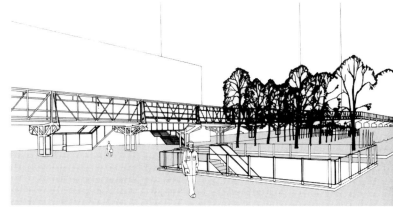

8.8
La Défense, Paris. Study made in 1975 for a moving pavement system to run elevated along the pedestrian deck. View along the enclosed tube which ramps down to deck level at either end.

8.9
View along deck with stairs and escalators up to intermediate access on left. The soffit of the tube follows closely that of the deck. Architect: Brian Richards. Consulting engineers: Ove Arup with Jean Prouve (Consultant).

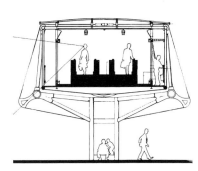

8.10
Cross section through tube showing supporting structure, designed by Peter Rice, with tension cables transferring loads down the circular columns. These are intended to relate to the surrounding avenue of trees. The glazing was designed to slide open by 50 per cent to reduce solar gain.

La Défense, a major sub-centre west of Paris (see p. 78) with a central deck over 1 km long has the main stations at one end, serving a working population of over 100,000 people. The requirement was for a moving pavement system to be provided as an aid to walking. The study by the author (see above) shows a glazed tube enclosing moving pavements 250 m and 172 m long running low above the deck, ramping at each end to deck level with one intermediate entry point. Traditional greenhouse technology would be used to open 50 per cent of the glazing, to reduce heat gain. The scheme was finally replaced by a metro, running below the deck linking into the Paris metro.

The 1978 Adelaide Study, for Dunlop, by the author (see p. 67) was a study for the local authority, to show how moving pavements could be integrated into a specific street. The requirements of the various authorities, fire, police or servicing, required evaluating different locations. A ground-level system, running in city block lengths, which gave the best travel times, also proved to be the most economic location and most convenient for pedestrians.

The Skywalk built for the Hanover Expo 2000 (pp. 108–111) remains a permanent feature and forms a dramatic link between the rail station and the exhibition grounds, designed by architects Schulitz and Partner with RFR Structural engineers, Paris.

8.11
Hanover, Germany, Expo 2000. The 340 m long elevated Skywalk connecting the railway station to the exhibition grounds. View of the tube outside, showing the integration of lighting with the structure.

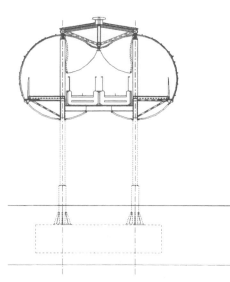

8.12
Structural cross section of the Skywalk showing the truss at the top, spanning 20–28 m, on to supporting columns. This allows for the curved laminated glass windows to be uninterrupted. Natural ventilation is by linear openings at the roof apex and at the bottom of the glazing. Architects: Helmut Schulitz and Partner. Structural engineers: RFR, Paris.

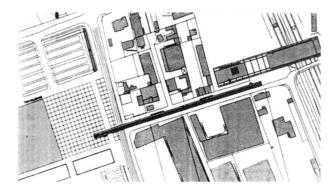

8.13
Plan showing the 340 m long Skywalk, elevated along Munchener Strasse, uniting a fragmented building frontage. Architects: Helmut Schulitz and Partner. Structural engineers: RFR, Paris.

8.14 *below*
View at the end of the tube adjacent to the railway platforms showing access by lift, escalators and stairs.

8.15 *overleaf*
Hanover Skywalk. Internal view of the tube showing 2 m wide curved glazing. Natural ventilation is by linear openings at the bottom and at roof level, supplemented in hot weather by mechanical means.

New developments   In the period 1970–76 development by the Battelle Institute, for Dunlop, adopted a highly original platform configuration, driven by electricity, based on the principle of fluids, which move slowly where they are running in a wide channel and fast when the channel is narrow. Called Speed-away, now being developed in Japan by Mitsubishi, this system accelerates passengers to three times the entry speed, decelerating them in the same way as they leave the system at the end.

Two further systems are being developed in Japan – the Accel-Liner (see Figures 8.16, 8.18) by Ishikawajima-Harima, and the Loderway invented by John Loder an Australian engineer, by Fujitec. These enable speeds of up to 4 times the entry speed to be attained. With these systems, longer distances can be covered at speeds more than double that of walking. In practice, passengers will not be encouraged to walk on them to avoid the problems of them 'bunching together' as they decelerate at the end of the system. Moving pavements are proposed for Singapore's Marina South development (see p. 65) which will aid pedestrian movement. In this development they will be installed in stages, as the size of the development enlarges and will carry passengers from the proposed two new subway stations.

8.16
Accel-Liner, a high-speed moving pavement system developed in Japan. This shows the individual platforms which overlap at the beginning and end and extend through the fast zone.

8.17
Melbourne, Australia. View of Loderway, a high-speed moving pavement system using belts, moving through rollers at varying speeds and butted close together.

8.18
Workshop view of Accel-Liner showing it running through a gradual curve. Courtesy: Ishikawajika-Harima Heavy Industries.

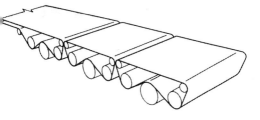

8.19
Diagram of Loderway showing principle of belts running through a tight radius and end-to-end to give acceleration. Courtesy: Fujitec, Japan.

City cars

The city car ideally is a vehicle which takes up a small amount of space when parked and is designed to be easily driven within a city's streets. Such a vehicle might be either privately owned, or capable of being hired for short distance travel, when a personal vehicle is useful, such as when packages have to be carried. Drivers would be members of a 'club' which gave them access to city cars at designated parking places, paying for the time they use the car or the distance driven. This idea was first tried in the 1970s in France, using a standard small car and in Holland where a specially made electric car, the Witkar, was used. Both experiments were, however, of too small a scale to show their capability and it was not until the 1980s that 'car share clubs' really began in earnest. These were not related to the city car concept but used a range of standard cars.

Today car sharing is developing in two directions. The city car, or 'smart car' club, largely developed experimentally by Japanese car manufacturers, uses an electric car of small scale, available for short trips, by many different drivers in any one day. In contrast to this is the 'car share club' of which over 60,000 members exist in Europe. This provides a range of vehicle sizes at points in a city for its members who pre-book the vehicle for use for as long as it is required.

Smart car clubs   At least three Japanese car manufacturers, Honda, Toyota and Nissan, are now developing sophisticated on-board intelligent management systems, which identify, for example, the position of each car at a central control centre, and whether its battery is in need of charging up. Club members with 'smart' cards can book the vehicles by phone or at parking points, using the vehicles as required. An important experiment in the San Francisco area in 1999, sponsored by Honda, used 15 of their standard Civic four-person cars, adapted for liquid gas (LPG), each equipped with 'intelligent' technology allowing it to be tracked by the central control. Two stations on the Bay Area Rapid Transit (BART) system were provided with priority parking for the vehicles, for use by any of the 38 car club members using smart cards. The cars could be used in any of three different ways: for the driver's sole use; shared with a car-pooler; or for short-term hourly use during the day. Thus a car driven to a station might be booked by another driver for use during the day, returning it to the station in the evening. The experiment showed that thirty of the club members were attracted into using the rail line for commuting to work, who would otherwise have driven all the way, and that some would have given up owning a second car.

Toyota, in their factory grounds outside Tokyo, are today using a fleet of 50 electric cars called Crayon, serving 700 personnel operating from 13 stations (see

Figure 8.20), where their batteries are charged. Their personnel have access to the vehicles using smart cards and return them to the original charging station after use.

Honda in their Intelligent Community Vehicle System (ICVS) programme have been testing a 'family of systems', four different vehicles ranging from electric bicycles to two-person cars (see p. 116). These will be available to club members at any 'port terminal' within a city, with the use of a smart card. The vehicles are intended to be left at any terminal for use by other drivers. This idea requires that the vehicles are redistributed, between terminals, with manpower required to move the vehicles around, ensuring that each terminal has a supply of vehicles available (see also 'Smart bikes', see Figure 8.33).

In 1999 Suzuki and Nissan started experimenting in a real-life situation with 50 electric cars in a dense business area, one kilometre square, of Yokohama. Ten stations are used with around 100 members, given free use of the cars, including

8.20
Charging point for Crayon cars. Members are billed for the time they use each car.

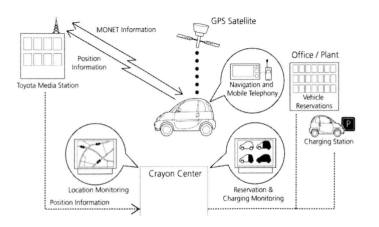

8.21 *above*
View of five-car charging station for electric Crayon car by Toyota. Thirteen stations are located in the factory grounds serving 700 employees who are car club members.

8.22
Crayon cars use metal hydride batteries which can be quickly charged. Each car has a navigation system determining their location and informs a driver if he strays from a zone. Courtesy: Toyota Eco Project.

8.23
Honda's experimental Intelligent Community Vehicle System (ICVS). The project tested four specially developed types of vehicle. View of electric power-assisted bicycle (Raccoon) stand and charging point.

8.24
View of four one-person electric cars (Mon Pal) for short-distance trips.

8.25
Automatic charging arm for City Pal car. Courtesy: Honda Motor Co.

8.26
View of charging station for 2 two-person electric cars (City Pal).

8.27
Nissan's experimental Urban Rental System in
Yokohama, Japan. View showing their Altra
electric vehicles being charged up. Four Altras
take up the space of 10 standard sized cars.

Relocation solution by IT

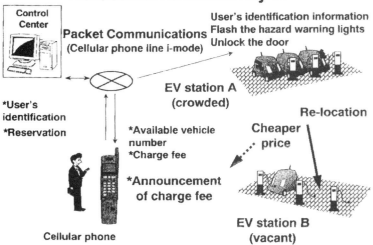

8.28
Nissan's proposed relocation system allowing
drivers to leave cars at any station if space is
available. Alternatively they are told by mobile
phone where parking space is available.
Courtesy: Nissan Motor Co.

the tiny Nissan Altra EV vehicle (see Figure 8.27). Each member is provided with a personal transmitter instead of a smart card, with which they can book a car, unlock its doors and use it. So far the results of driver surveys appear favourable, although the control staff could handle up to 300 cars which would reduce operating costs. Parking was found to be an important factor in this busy section of the city, with four Nissan Altra EVs taking the space of 10 normal-sized cars, saving over £120 monthly per vehicle.

A fleet of 'managed' electric vehicles could be used within a large new development, such as that proposed by the Architect Isosaki in his Mirage City (see Figures 8.29, 8.30). Here a single supplier could be under contract to supply and maintain a fleet of electric vehicles, used for both the movement of people as well as servicing. This occurred in the Sydney Olympics, where the main site was made car-free, with servicing by a fleet of 370 electric vehicles, supplied by a British manufacturer, Frazer Nash Research. The vehicles were specially designed, ranging from small police cars and fire trucks to trailer buses and tractors, all of which could have their batteries charged within 40 minutes, with some using a back-up of solar powered panels on their roofs (see p. 119).

Today electric cars are expensive, partly because they are not yet in mass production, but also because they are designed to run at high speeds in order to be marketable. If their speeds were governed, to a maximum of 50 kph (30 mph) or less,

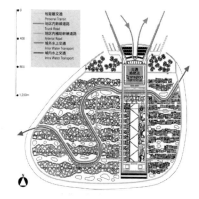

8.29
Mirage City, China, 1995. A Utopian project for an artificial island at Haishi, off Macau, in the South China Sea, intended as a centre of international exchange. Plan showing the entry roads from the mainland serving the transport terminal where all external vehicles park. Movement within the island is to be on foot, by cycles with electric cars, and by boat.

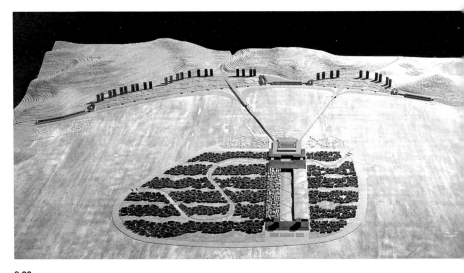

8.30
View of the model. Courtesy: Arata Isosaki, Architect.

(a)

(b)

(c)

(d)

8.31
Sydney Olympics, 2000, Australia. Planned by a team led by architect Lawrence Nield to be a car-free site. The servicing was done by a fleet of 370 specially designed electric vehicles. The battery design allowed an almost full charge in 30–40 minutes. Some vehicles had roof-mounted solar panels, giving a 10 per cent increase in range. (a) trailer bus carried 30 competitors from the Olympic Village; (b) fire truck; (c) police van; (d) tractor with trailer for work within the stadium. Courtesy: Frazer Nash Research Ltd.

8.32
The 'Think' electric car, a two-seater manufactured in Norway, uses a cadmium battery-powered engine with a 10-year life giving it an 85 km (53 mile) range on one charge. Three metres long, the car has thermoplastic body panels. Courtesy: 'Think' & Ford Motor Co.

this would help reduce their cost, and make them safer for pedestrians within built-up areas (Plowden, 1980). Their battery design, too, has been much improved. Ford, for example, has now purchased a factory in Norway, manufacturing the 'Think' electric car, a vehicle with a 10-year battery life and a range of 85 km (53 miles). This is more than enough distance to make it an ideal vehicle for car clubs to use.

Smart bikes   In 1998 the city of Rennes, northern France, with a population of 340,000 people, started a system of 'smart bike' hire. Developed by Adshel, an advertising company, the system in Rennes consists of 25 'docking stations' located at key generation points, such as at the train station or shopping centres,

8.33
Rennes, France. View of 'smart bike' docking station. Bikes can be taken by club members by
inserting an access card into the individual console mounted on the docking rail. Cards are scanned
and checked by central computer. The bike released has to be returned within two hours to any
docking station. Rennes has 25 docking stations with free bikes used by 2,000 members. Over
40,000 trips, averaging 26 minutes, were made in 1999. Courtesy: Adshel.

situated within the neighbourhoods. At these points 200 bikes are located. Over
1,300 free smart cards were issued to residents and university students which
allow any available bike to be unlocked. The bicycle must be returned to any
docking station within a 2-hour period, unless a longer period is required. The
central computer stores information about who is using a bike, for how long, as
well as informing the driver of the 'dispatch vehicle' where any docking stations
are overloaded. Bikes are then redistributed as necessary by van to ensure an
even distribution.

In 1999 there were over 40,000 trips made by 'smart bike' in Rennes, with average trip lengths of around 26 minutes. A system has subsequently started in a dense neighbourhood of Singapore, Bukit Batok, serving apartment buildings. Here 860 members, who pay a refundable deposit for a card, are now using any of the 100 bikes located at the 10 docking stations, with between 40 and 50 per cent of trips being made to the local metro station or bus stops.

Car clubs   Car clubs are now well established in several European countries, including Germany, Switzerland and Holland. In Germany, a club called StattAuto (German for car alternative) now has 20,000 members and serves 18 cities with 1,000 cars of varying size, including the new Mercedes–Benz 'smart car'. Parking places, agreed with each local authority, are spaced at intervals around the city,

8.34
StattAuto, Germany. A car club with 20,000 members in 18 cities. View of typical station point where members insert their club card to obtain car keys. Courtesy: StattAuto.

8.35
'Smart' car launched by Mercedes–Benz in 1998. Cars are low-emission, two-seaters, 2.5 m long, and are for urban use. Courtesy: MCC Smart GmbH.

each with a safe box (see Figure 8.34). Cars are booked by phone or Internet and members are told where they are available. A magnetic 'smart card' releases the doors of a pre-booked car and provide the ignition key. The car is driven for an agreed time of one hour or more and the member leaves a written note on the distance driven which is collected later by maintenance staff and transferred to his or her monthly account at the control centre.

More complex and costly systems used in Hamburg and by Greenwheels in Holland have on-board equipment which automatically tells the central office when the car starts and how long it has been used. The Japanese systems also use global positioning satellites to show the control centre where each car is situated. Car clubs normally charge a flat annual fee to members and a charge per kilometre driven. This is still cheaper than actually owning a car. Members are those who often give up owning their own car or are family members who use the cars instead of purchasing a second car.

La Rochelle, France is operating experimentally a fleet of 50 modified electric small cars by Citroen and Peugeot. These are parked at six designated points around the town, between 2 and 5 km apart for the use of 400 registered members who pay a monthly subscription of around £3. Members use a smart card for opening the car's doors, punching their pin numbers into a keyboard which allows the car to start. A central computer is informed of the distance travelled, and by whom, and members are billed monthly through direct debit. Lights at the rear of each car show if it is reserved, free, or needs recharging by staff members. California's Air Resources Board intends to uphold the State Law which requires that 10 per cent of new cars sold in the state are electric by 2003. This has prompted the Japanese car manufacturers to develop EVs as well as Ford, mentioned above, with their 'Think' vehicle. Already a number of garages there have free charge points for electric cars. Other incentives, too, could be given, such as reducing their licence fee, or insurance, if their speeds were governed. Car clubs in the UK are only just beginning. In North America they are starting in those cities like Boston or Portland where public transport is good and where there is public concern for the environment and for being less car-dependent.

Car clubs, although the membership in Europe is growing, still represent a small proportion of total car owners and the profits for those that run them are not high. However, this may change as car ownership becomes progressively more expensive with parking within cities more difficult. Their main advantage, environmentally, is that their members do apparently drive less. A mobility car sharing study in Switzerland (Shaheen et al., 1999) showed that mileage driven by members who had previously owned their own cars reduced by 33–50 per cent. This may be due to their being more aware of 'paying as they drive', as well as on the quality of public transport available (Zurich's citizens use public transport an average of 800 times a year). If parking space is freed for other uses, as was done in the Edinburgh housing scheme, then they deserve public support. They undoubtedly give a greater degree of mobility for people who otherwise could not afford a car. However, car clubs do not reduce the necessity for a city to provide good public transport, as well, for those who do not drive.

Personal rapid transit

Even in the 1960s, the popularity of the private car and the degree of congestion on the roads in the United States, led the Department of Housing and Urban Development (HUD) to seek out alternative ideas for transport, from their research institutions, which would still hold on to the basic idea of using small individual vehicles.

One of the first ideas put forward was for a small car that could be used in a different way. In 1960 William Alden, an engineer, founded the Alden Self-Transit Systems Corporation in Bedford, Massachusetts, developing a dual-mode minicar, called a StarrCar. This was a two-seater car that could be driven on roads in the normal way, probably as a rented vehicle. For trips downtown or crosstown it would be driven to the nearest guideway entry station, where it would be carried under electric power, to enter an automatic parking garage and available for use by others, or off the track on to the local roads, and retained for the reverse trip.

By 1965 Alden had an operational vehicle and was working on a closed-loop system for Kennedy and other airports. The vehicle was designed to go on to the aprons, carrying a small container, and unload directly into planes. Similar ideas (see Figure 8.38) were shown in drawings made around the same time by Buck-minster Fuller, called 'the travelling cartridge' except that his vehicles would enter the plane and could couple up and run as trains on a fixed track. Alden proposed that each car would have an in-vehicle switch which could steer it out from a string of other cars, without affecting its speed. This used a simple mechanical device, with minimal on-board electronics to keep it reliable, controlled by a central computer.

Alden proposed that the system would grow over a 15–20 year period. It would start with an airport being first connected by guideway to downtown, then running out to the suburbs, connecting one metropolitan area with another (see Figure 8.37). Once the guideway was in place it could also handle small size containers. It is interesting to compare this with the Japanese CVS development which actually achieved this in its demonstration test-bed 10 years later (see p. 128).

In 1968 HUD published an influential transport paper called 'Future Urban Transportation Systems' by Stanford Research Institute which showed how a

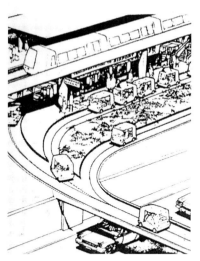

8.37
One of Alden's early sketches showing the automatic vehicle switching, on demand, into a station to allow passengers to interchange with a long-distance train. Courtesy: William Alden.

8.36
StarrCar developed in 1966 by William Alden. This system used small two-seater bi-modal cars, driven on local roads, or to the nearest entry point to the local guideway, where they would run automatically, computer-controlled, under electric power, to the required exit point. View of StarrCar running on local streets. Courtesy: William Alden.

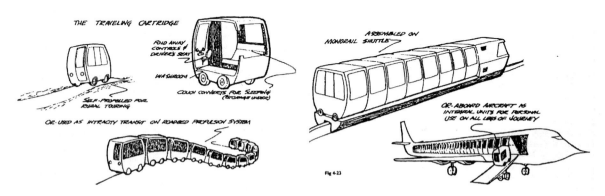

8.38
Buckminster Fuller's proposal for computerised personal transport using personal cabins. Passengers type their required destination into a computer at a station, insert their card and are driven automatically to their appropriate plane, which the cabin enters. From Baldwin's Bucky Works. Courtesy: John Wiley & Sons Inc.

whole 'family of systems', in the context of different urban densities, could evolve from ideas for dial-a-ride to peoplemovers. This report led to many firms in the US, Germany and France, developing small automatic vehicle systems. Many designs showed, on paper, that even small vehicles could, if they went fast enough, run close together and achieve prodigious capacities. In practice conservatism won the day and instead vehicles grew in size, as well as their supporting guideways (see Morgantown), in order to carry more passengers.

The first full-scale installation, which used Alden's switching system, was made in Morgantown, West Virginia, built to serve the University of West Virginia. This was financed through the US Department of Urban Development (HUD) and the Department of Transportation (UMTA). At Morgantown, Boeing managed the

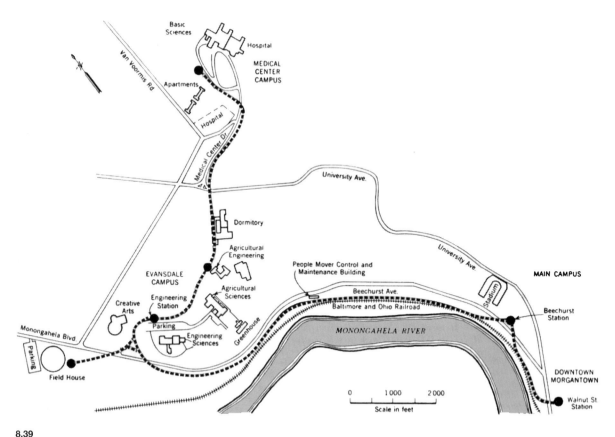

8.39
Morgantown, West Virginia. Site plan showing 8.8 km (5.5 mile) long guideway with six stations running in the valley, connecting with the university buildings.

8.40
View of cabins turning into a typical off-line station. Courtesy: The Boeing Company, Seattle.

8.41
View from inside cabin, carrying up to 21 passengers, looking along track.

8.42
View of typical station platform showing level boarding. Cabins are programmed through the central computer to run automatically, on demand, or on a regular basis according to the time of day, taking passengers to their required station with no intermediate stops.

construction of a 5-mile-long guideway, with 21-person vehicles, running up a steep valley, connecting the university buildings, previously served by 16 shuttle buses. Morgantown opened in 1975 and today carries 15,000 passengers a day, with an average trip distance of 1.5 miles.

It is programmed to operate in ways, according to need, either on demand, in scheduled operation, or in circulation mode. Running costs are around $3 million a year, subsidised by the University, with low fares at $1.5. Today, Morgantown is the only fully automated group transit system in public operation in the US. However, the environmental impact of the system is questionable, particularly along streets where the elevated guideway runs, with a deep cross section and stations unnecessarily large compared with the Japanese CVS system.

In 1968 the Japanese developed their computer-controlled vehicle system (CVS). First, as a 'traffic game' at the Osaka Expo, using several dozen electric two-person minicars, like dodgem cars, running automatically on a checkerboard, guided by floor grooves, with intersections every 5 m. Subsequently, by 1970, a

8.43
Computer-controlled vehicle system (CVS). Overall view of test facility. This shows how a wide range of operations were possible. On the right is the automatic container-handling facility and a typical off-line station. The central guidance system permitted cabin turns to be made within a tight radius.

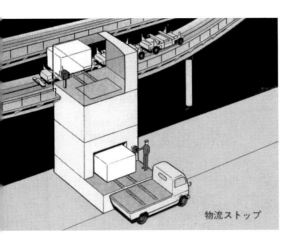

物流ストップ

8.44
Proposed goods handling system. Special container-carrying vehicles would load and unload automatically in a lay-by and be transported by lift to an unloading bay serving road vehicles.

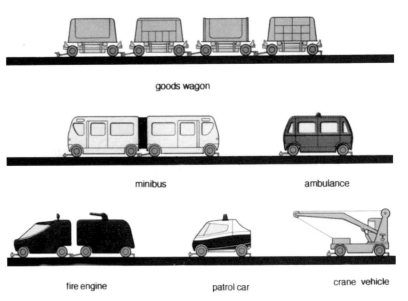

goods wagon

minibus

ambulance

fire engine

patrol car

crane vehicle

8.45
A range of vehicle types could be used on the track. A city could potentially be planned which would allow all vehicle operations to be automatically controlled. Courtesy: Mechanical Social Systems Foundation.

team of engineers and architects, sponsored by the Ministry of International Trade and Industry (MITI), developed a 4.8 km test track or guideway grid on which any number of permutations were possible. The vehicles included freight carriers, with docks at platforms for automatic loading and unloading (see p. 128). Vehicles carried four people, and could turn on the guideway in a 5 m radius. Development was subsequently halted and the system placed on hold, in favour of studies into automated freeways and high-tech cars.

Group rapid transit   Following the demise of personal rapid transit came the development of larger vehicles capable of being programmed to run to specific stations as required, and into sidings as described above for Morgantown. The most comprehensive and interesting installation is the Airtrans system installed at Dallas, Fort Worth, airport in 1974. This uses 42-passenger vehicles running on a 13-mile-long guideway. This runs partly at ground level, and sections are also elevated, with 53 stations. Some vehicles were designed to take 'Thunderbird' style pods to carry baggage, mail, supplies and even refuse (Warren, 1998). The system is running today and is about to be updated and although it required extensive 'debugging' when built it was still remarkable.

The development of automated shuttle systems for carrying people out to satellite boarding points at airports today operates worldwide. These are normally

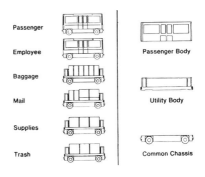

8.46
Various 'pods' are used on a standard chassis. Passenger vehicles carry 45 people and other pods handle goods of different kinds, such as baggage, refuse or supplies. Courtesy: LTV Aerospace Corporation.

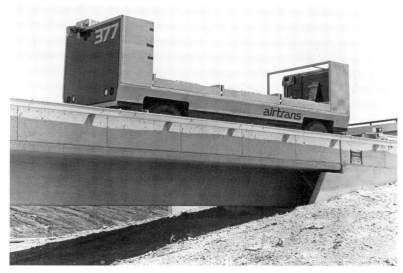

8.47
Dallas, Fort Worth, airport transit system, installed in 1974 and served 53 stations.

simple A to B systems over distances of up to 800 m, considered too far for conventional moving pavements. All the systems run on rubber tyres, on concrete guideways, elevated or underground, under electric power and computer control, but their high cost has reduced their use in urban situations. Singapore, for example, uses an automated shuttle at Bukit Panjang New Town, a 13 km long system with 19 stations serving the dense housing development. Each station is a short walk from each block and runs in a figure-of-eight loop connecting with the MRT rapid transit station serving downtown. The problem of overlooking has been dealt with by using special glass which becomes frosted as it passes close to the apartments. A further system has been installed in the centre of Miami and connects with the regional rail system and carries 22,000 passengers a day (Warren, 1998).

Horizontal elevators and peoplemovers   Simplified shuttle systems have been developed by Otis, who have been building lifts since Elisha Otis invented the first safety elevator in 1853 and founded the company. Their first vehicle was called Hovair, installed at Duke University, to link two medical centres, a distance of under 400 m. The vehicles float on an air cushion, both to reduce friction, allow the vehicle to move sideways and dock at stations, as well as provide a surface which does not need heating, or the need to clear it of snow and ice, which is required at Morgantown. The system at Duke was installed in 1977, uses 22 passenger vehicles, is driven by linear electric drive and is running today.

Subsequent installations have retained the air-cushion suspension, but adopt Alpine rail technology, using cable drive, to reduce costs. The Getty Foundation building, by Richard Meir architect (see Figure 8.49) in Los Angeles, uses the Otis shuttle. This starts from a terminal station above the 6-level parking building, adjoining the freeway. It climbs around 70 m, up the hillside to the Getty Centre, on a single lane guideway, with an intermediate passing point, and carries 1,200 people an hour in each direction. This is an example of how this technology has been used to separate drivers from their vehicles, which is difficult in Los Angeles and it appears to be popular with passengers.

Another simpler installation by Poma-Otis is at the Mystic Transportation Centre outside Boston. Here two-car shuttles, each carrying 45 passengers, run elevated over a rail yard, linking a car park and office complex in less than one minute over a distance of 238 m (see Figure 8.49). Travel speeds are up to 40 kph (25 mph) and up to 10 million passengers a year are carried. This is a typical urban situation showing the potential for a shuttle system, used in a situation where distances are too remote for walking, and too long for a conventional-speed moving pavement.

This section has explored the range of small-scale urban systems which have

8.48
Mystic Transportation Centre near Boston, Massachusetts. View shows two-car 45-person cabins, cable-driven, running from the parking building on a 25 m long elevated guideway to link with the railway station. The system has a capacity of 1,600 persons/hr in each direction and 10 million people a year are carried. Courtesy: Poma-Otis.

8.49

Los Angeles, California. The Getty Foundation, situated on a hill, is served by driverless three-car trains, built by Otis, which float on air cushions and are driven by cable. These run from the terminal, with parking below for 2,000 cars, climbing 70 m up to the Foundation at the top. The trains run every five minutes, carrying 1,200 passengers an hour in each direction. View of terminus at plaza level serving the Foundation buildings. Passengers leave and board the trains from opposite sides.

250 500   1000 feet

Overall Site Plan

8.50

Site plan showing vehicle entrance off the Freeway at top left, with parking for 2,000 cars. Courtesy: Richard Meir, Architect.

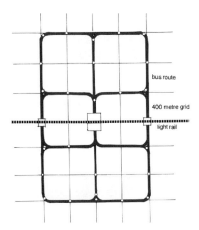

8.51
Diagram showing how light-rail stops at 800 m intervals would serve a residential area with dense mixed development around alternate stops. Feeder buses serving the housing areas would have stops at 300–400 m intervals. Each would serve around 1,600 people at a density of 100 persons/ha.

8.52
Glendale, California. Two examples of the devices used by passengers to get actual arrival times for buses at their local stops: by wireless on their (WAP) mobile phones or through their Palm Internet device. Courtesy: Nextbus Information Systems Inc.

been tried in the last 30 years. Many have influenced airport planning, allowing airports to extend dramatically where funds for such systems are readily available. So far their effect on urban planning has been negligible, due to their high cost and also the conservatism of transport authorities to experiment with new technology.

The future of buses

Buses of varying sizes, according to demand, will continue to be the basic system of public transport for reasons of their flexibility and cost. In order to be economic to run within residential areas, densities of around 100 persons/ha will be necessary (UTF), a figure that will vary between affluent areas where car ownership is high, to areas which might be car-free from choice. The road layout is a critical factor and roads must be laid out on continuous routes rather than with cul-de-sacs (see Figure 1.7).

Buses will circulate or distribute passengers within local areas as well as serving local centres. These centres would be a point where shops and other facilities are sited, in some cases adjoining a rail station or light-rail stop, running to the city centre. The diagram (see Figure 8.51) shows a residential area with a density of 100 persons/ha served by buses connecting with three light-rail stops, one of which might have denser development around it. Cross-town trips are more complex, but important, and entail passengers interchanging on to other routes. How convenient this is depends on systems called 'timed transfer' used in Edmonton, Canada (see Figure 8.83). Here, a high proportion of trips are to cross-town destinations, rather than to downtown and car ownership is relatively low. Every bus is identified through satellite positioning at a central control room, ensuring that it arrives on time at interchange stops. Waiting time for passengers is minimal and they can cross platforms on to other buses. Portland, Oregon has implemented eight timed transfer stations and restructured part of its road system in order to make this work.

Reliability of service is an important factor, and if road congestion is serious and sufficient buses are run, priority lanes will be necessary to ensure that they can run on time. If not, then passengers must be informed when a bus will arrive at a stop. London, by 2005, will have 25 per cent of its busiest stops equipped with 'Countdown' boards (some 4,500) each connected to a central computer with roadside beacons feeding information on the position of each bus, showing when it will arrive at a stop. A development of this is now being tried by a California company, Nextbus, in the San Francisco region. It uses global positioning satellites (GPS) to locate each bus position on a route in Glendale, relaying this information to 'real-time' boards at 150 stops. In addition, passengers with compatible mobile phones, or through the Internet, on their paging devices (see Figure 8.52),

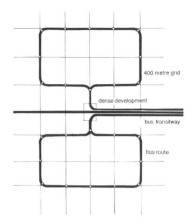

8.53

Diagram showing a bus transitway where buses circulate within residential areas before entering the transitway where they proceed to the city centre without the need for interchanging.

8.54

View of Ottawa's Transitway showing local buses serving fully enclosed bus stops with through express buses passing through en route for downtown. Courtesy: Ottawa-Carleton Commission.

are given information on bus arrival times at a stop. This allows them to sit at home, shop or wait in their office lobby before being advised when it is time to walk to their local stop – a boon in wintry weather or where a service is either erratic or infrequent.

These are some of the factors that will help determine whether buses can provide a service within residential areas which compares favourably with, and is an attractive alternative to, the private car.

Curitiba, Brazil, uses express bus transit running on separate lanes along the centre of the five principal boulevards radiating from the city centre (see Figure 2.2). Stops every 1,400 m are designed to allow passengers to interchange with local feeder or interdistrict (see Figure 8.87) buses and still remain within the ticketed area, with a single fare valid for all trips. The circular tube bus stops (see Figure 2.3) can handle twice as many passengers per hour as a conventional stop, because of level boarding (Newman and Kenworthy).

Ottawa-Carleton, Canada, relies on a specially built, separate road system called the Transitway, situated largely in a cutting, 12 miles long with 30 weather-protected stops along it. Buses circulate within the low-density residential areas before entering the Transitway (see Figure 8.53) and run at high speeds downtown without the need for passengers interchanging. It is in the downtown area, however, that problems occur because of the high number of buses. Unlike Curitiba where the downtown is simply banned to cars, in the centre of Ottawa there is insufficient lane space or kerb length to unload in the rush hour, added to which cars frequently use these lanes.

Guided buses   Three manufacturers in Europe are developing guided buses as an alternative system to trams. These are intended to be cheaper than trams by being lighter in weight and so reduce the costs of guideways and the need for roads to be strengthened, which for trams can cost from £2 million upwards per km (Hass-Klau et al., 2000). The aim is to run on a conventional road bed with a width reduced from that normally required for a two-way busway of 9 m to around 6.7 m. Alstom is experimenting with electric cable guidance using two buried cables under the road surface. Matra is using optical guidance, following a painted line on the road. Bombardier is using a single guidance rail in the middle of the track. Overhead wires for all three systems provide electric power and if the buses are to leave the track, to circulate within surrounding areas, a second motor is required which adds to their weight. The intention is that guidance allows drivers to bring the bus close to the raised stops for wheelchair access, similar to a low-floor tram. Only one system, the O'Bahn developed by Daimler-Benz in 1970 for the Federal German Government, is today in operation. This uses a standard bus with three side guidance wheels on either side, connected with the power

8.55
Translohr lightweight tram, estimated by manufacturers Lohr to cost 50 per cent less than a conventional vehicle through use of an aluminium chassis. Runs on rubber tyres, central guided with possible onboard batteries, allowing it to run limited distances on existing streets. Now undergoing trials. Courtesy: Lohr Industrie.

8.56
Essen, Germany. The Essen-Kray 4 km long O'Bahn guided busway running in the centre section of the motorway. This uses side guidance wheels running against a raised concrete kerb. Courtesy: Daimler-Chrysler.

steering. The wheels bear against two concrete kerbs, 180 mm high set 2.6 m apart with breaks in the guideway to allow for pedestrians to cross (Figure 8.56).

Today around 26 km (16 miles) of guided busway exists worldwide, with the longest in Adelaide, South Australia. Here a two-way guideway 19 km long serves 10 bus routes, converging on to the end of the busway, carrying 12,000 passengers a day, one-way, with journey time reduced from 33 to 23 minutes. Leeds, England, has installed a short experimental one-way guideway, where buses can bypass traffic waiting at lights. This has proved to be so popular with the private operators that they now pay for fitting guidance wheels at a cost of £3,000 per bus (see Figure 8.66).

However, guideways using raised side kerbs cannot be used in pedestrian-only areas. The Bombardier guided bus uses a single guidance rail set into the ground

8.57
Adelaide, South Australia. The 19 km (12 mile) long busway runs through linear park and 10 bus routes converge at the outer end. This carries around 58 buses/hr at peak – around 12,000 passengers a day – reducing journey times from 33 to 23 minutes to the centre. Courtesy: North-east Busway project team, Adelaide.

8.58
Nancy, France. Bombardier GLT Guided buses, use single retractable central bogies set into the road bed with an overhead catenary. Courtesy: Bombardier Transport.

8.59
The Bombardier low-floor vehicle can carry up to 165 passengers – 68 seated and 97 standing – and run at speeds of up to 80 kph (50 mph). Boarding shown at platform level.

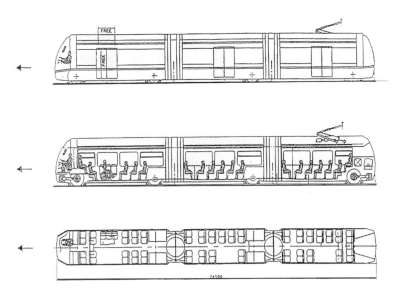

8.60
Drawings showing layout of typical vehicle with space for two wheelchairs.

and is operating in Nancy, France, replacing the existing trolley buses (see p. 136). Guided buses, ideally, require a special concrete roadbed to provide a smooth ride (see p. 139) at only slightly less cost than that required for a tram. They have the flexibility to leave the end of the guideway and circulate within residential areas, as they do in Adelaide. But a guideway can carry only about 60 buses an hour safely in each direction. It is still too early to predict whether the new guided buses under development (see Figure 8.55) will be seen by the public to be as attractive a means of travel as light rail and can afford as comfortable a ride.

Central areas   Cities which solely use bus transport, because of their limited capacity, frequently experience problems of congestion in their central areas unless separate roads are assigned for their exclusive use. The original Transitway, in Portland, Oregon carried up to 175 buses during the peak hours until they were replaced by a light rail system. Ottawa, discussed above, has severe problems with congested streets in its centre, which have not been given over for exclusive bus use. Cities which remain car-oriented have this problem, politically, and are reluctant to give over downtown streets or pedestrian-only areas for the exclusive use of buses. In addition, buses in the past have been a source of noise and fumes, although fuel cell buses, if successful, could change this. At present light

8.61
Seattle, Washington. The 2 km long bus subway with five stations crossing below the city centre was built in 1987, carries dual-mode buses away from surface streets which are full of traffic. Half the estimated $80 million cost was funded by the Federal Government. View along typical station where dual-mode buses run under electric power and on diesel power outside the subway.

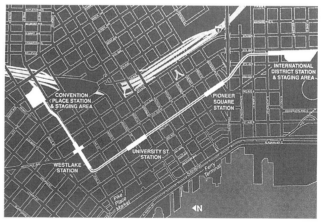

8.62
T Bus subway plan shows a direct connection into the freeway bus-only and HOV (high occupancy vehicle) lanes. Courtesy: Metro.

8.63
Montpellier, France. Interchange at Corum station in the centre showing high-level glazed roof providing weather protection to passengers interchanging from local buses on right (le petit bus) on to light rail on left.

rail is seen to be more pedestrian-friendly than buses and compatible with pedestrian areas, as well as carry more people. One way of dealing with buses in a city centre was tried at Seattle, Washington where a 2 km long cavernous subway was built (see Figure 8.61) with three stations at a reputed cost of $46 million, built with Federal funds at a time when only buses were receiving grants. The buses in this subway will shortly be replaced by a light rail which would be far better run at surface level.

Vehicles   A range of bus sizes operate in cities according to the needs of each route. Within dense historic areas, with narrow streets, special city buses are often used, with low floors, carrying 28 passengers. These buses are less than 6 m long and can turn on a tight radius of 7 m. Florence, for example, runs a fleet of electric buses from its main line station into the pedestrian area. Montpellier uses the 'petit bus' of similar size, running within traffic-free areas at 10 minute intervals. These stop to pick up, or drop passengers, on demand and interchange with a tram stop under a glass-covered roof (see Figure 8.63). Increasingly in the future this kind of small, flexible, attractive vehicle will be used in urban areas, although it is costly to run, in terms of manpower. Their integration at Montpellier with the principal system of trams and their ready availability suggests that car access to tram stops in some situations can be eliminated.

8.64
Montpellier. Plan showing routes of 'petit bus'. These serve narrow residential streets in the historic area and drop or pick up on demand at 10-minute intervals. Courtesy: TAM.

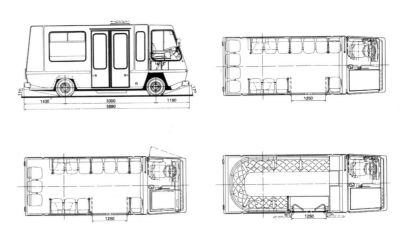

8.65
'Le petit bus' originally made by the Austrian firm Steyr. A small low-floored vehicle with wide double doors carrying up to 30 passengers. Plan showing alternative internal layouts to suit requirements. Courtesy: Steyr/Volvo.

8.66
Leeds, England. Level boarding at a typical bus stop on short guided sections allows buses to pass vehicles held back at street junctions. Private bus companies are financing guidance to be fitted to buses. Courtesy: West Yorkshire PTA & Metro.

Curitiba, Brazil, uses a range of nine sizes of bus, serving different areas of the city, carrying from 30 people, with duo-articulated Volvo express buses carrying 270 passengers. None of these buses uses low-floored vehicles, probably due to their cost, and as a result stops have been designed with raised floors, to the express buses, with lifts required for the disabled at each stop. Generally manufacturers are now all making low-floored vehicles, around 340 mm above ground level. Even with raised stops, some form of short ramp is often used. The time saved at stops with buses with low floors is now seen to justify their high cost. Vehicle life of buses is generally around 10 years. Curitiba replaces its express buses every three years. This compares with the 25–30 year life of a tram. However, the cost of a bus which carries 80 passengers is still around one-fifth of the cost of a tram carrying 250 passengers, costing around £1.2 million per vehicle.

The design of the road bed is an important factor affecting the riding conditions of buses. The O'Bahn guided bus, discussed above, affords a good ride because it runs on a precast concrete bed with less likelihood of the 'rutting' which can occur on a conventional road surface. Although the new guided vehicles shown (see Figure 8.55) may be two-thirds the weight of a tram, they may still require special road surfaces in order to give a good ride. In theory by being light, it may mean that no changes are needed to underground services, which with a tram system on existing roads can cost £5 million per km. In new development the route of services will be preplanned and this problem will not occur. If guided buses are to be successful in replacing trams in the future, the quality of ride will have to be comparable, as will other factors such as the quality of their design.

Design   At present there has been too little demand from bus operators to commission industrial designers to improve bus design. Operators are given a choice of seat colour, rarely good, and the introduction of low floors has been the only real innovation in recent years. Exceptions to this are the new buses designed for the RATP in Paris by one of France's best known designers, Roger Tallon, also responsible for the fine interiors of the Meteor underground trains. Hanover's transport operator USTRA is another operator supporting good design and commissioned two British designers – Jasper Morrison for a new tram, the TW2000, and James Irvine for two sizes of bus, the Stadtbus (see p. 141). Both these were put into production for the 2000 Expo, remain part of the transport fleet and received high design awards.

The design of the new guided buses under trial in France is also a step forward, for example, the stylish Translohr system (see Figure 8.55) by the Italian coachbuilder Parizzi. Bus operators in the future, if they are to be successful in attracting people to use them, require imaginative new designs of this kind to help encourage people back onto them.

The new fuels   Buses which previously ran on diesel fuel are now becoming 'cleaner' either using a cleaner fuel and filters which remove some of the particulates. Progress has been made in the United States, with Federal funds available from the Department of Energy, to encourage bus companies to run cleaner vehicles, using liquid or propane gas, or hybrid vehicles, using motors which keep electric batteries charged up for use within central areas.

8.67
Fuel-cell bus by Ballard and Xcellsis, undergoing two-year trial by Sunline bus company in Palm Springs, California. Sole emissions are water drips from pipe at bottom and water vapour through exhaust pipe at top of bus. Liquid hydrogen shown being filled into tank from pump. Lighter and more compact developments of fuel cells are expected to reduce costs substantially.

The single largest breakthrough in motive power expected is the fuel cell, which could be the power source of the future. This produces zero emissions, only water vapour, with low maintenance and a reduced noise level. Fuel cells either require liquid hydrogen as fuel, obtained from natural gas, or methanol. This is combined with oxygen from the air, which is free, to generate electricity which drives the vehicle. Special pumps running from storage tanks are required for dispensing hydrogen.

Once private cars start using fuel cells, only a few are running at present, hydrogen would rapidly be available from any filling station. At present field trials with six buses by Ballard and Xcellsis use a lighter engine than the first models.

8.68

Generous spaces provided for pushchairs, wheelchairs and baggage.

8.69

An articulated low-floored bus, the Stadtbus, designed by James Irvine for the Hanover Transport Authority, USTRA and built by Mercedes. Carries 152 people and uses natural gas or diesel power. The deep roof carries the air-conditioning plant. A fleet of 101 of these were originally built for Expo 2000 and are now part of the bus fleet. Courtesy: USTRA.

8.70

Plan of 18 m long low-floor articulated Stadtbus. Single door at front for passengers buying a ticket from the driver and two double doors behind the front axle with extending ramps opening into an area (the Piazza) with space for wheelchairs, prams or baggage.

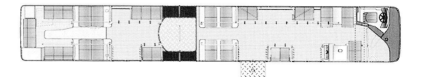

This has reduced the original cost by 50 per cent within the last two years, making them similar to that of a trolley bus. Further work is continuing to reduce this cost still further. Daimler-Benz will shortly be starting trials of 30 buses in six European cities, including London, with EEC funding. If these prove successful, this will substantially help to improve the image of buses as transport for the future.

Future light rail systems

The importance of light rail systems lies in their ability to attract passengers back to using public transport (see p. 13). European cities of 250,000 people, now under intense pressure from cars, have generally made at least part of their centres car-free, crossed by light rail, with much of the parking moved to the periphery. Strasbourg, for example, with a centre previously crossed by 50,000 cars daily, many of which were searching for parking, has instead removed 2,000 parking spaces from the centre to park-and-ride points outside (Hass-Klau *et al.*, 2000). As streets have been cleared of vehicles, to make way for light rail, there has also been an effort made to improve the quality of design of the city streets through which it passes.

Urban design   The insertion of light rail, notably in France, is now being done with considerable attention to detail. Grenoble in 1987 was the first city to redesign trams with low floors 250 mm above ground level for disabled access with the stops, in some cases, raised to the same level as the pavement. At the same time the entire central area streets were paved with many of them for pedestrian-only use. The cost of these environmental improvements is reflected in the costs involved, for the first line built. The cost of the tramway itself, a 9 km (6 mile) long route, was approximately £58 million. The transport improvements were £15 million. The traffic alterations were £14 million and £30 million was spent on improvements, such as street paving. The message here is that light rail, properly integrated into the street environment, does not come cheap. The present day costs for a two-way system can vary between £3 million and £10 million per km, excluding vehicles costing between one and two million pounds each. Added to these costs should be figures comparable to those given for Grenoble where a city has built a system which actually ends up improving the whole street scene.

Lyons, although not closing the city centre to cars, is reducing car use in some areas, giving priority to light rail movement in the centre. For example, the square opposite the main Part-Dieu railway station, is for buses and trams, and Avenue Berthelot, previously a six-lane boulevard carrying 45,000 cars a day, is narrowed

8.71
Portland, Oregon. View of typical street crossing on the transit mall where road finishes identify the presence of the tram tracks for pedestrians. Photo: Strode Eckert. Architects: Zimmer, Gunsul, Frasca Partnership.

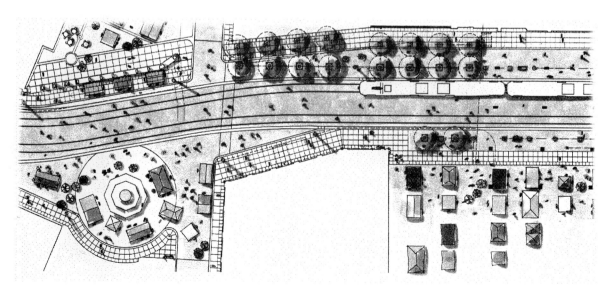

8.72
Portland, Oregon. Detail of landscaping and pavement layout adjoining light-rail track. Courtesy: Tri-Met.

8.73
Bordeaux, France. Computer montage of typical street in city centre showing intended integration of light rail. Access by vehicles shown reduced with single lane provided on right. Courtesy: Communauté Urbaine de Bordeaux-Mission Tramway. Architects: Brochet, Lajus, Pueyo.

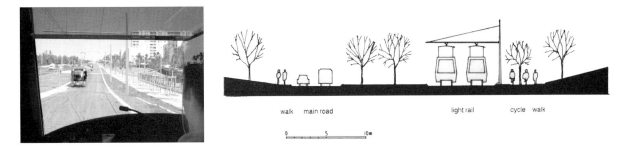

8.74
Montpellier, France. Typical wide suburban boulevard within new residential area showing grassed area between tracks and new trees planted on right to shade cycleway.

to be one-way, with trams in the centre, with an avenue of 300 lime trees planted alongside. Landscaping, in France, is now considered to be an important factor, when building any new light rail line. Those cities building new lines are proud of their achievements in transforming their fabric, previously torn apart by the private car. Strasbourg, for example, planted over 1,000 trees, to soften part of one route. In Paris the 9 km long peripheral line, built on the boulevard between Bobigny and St Denis, has been reduced to two lanes, with plane trees planted continuously on either side of the tracks. Laying turf between tracks is standard practice. In Montpellier this is particularly effective in the suburbs, where the green band of turf between the lines links, visually, to the green areas on either side (see Figure 8.74).

Bordeaux has commissioned architects and landscape architects who are studying the streets where light rail will run, producing computerised drawings to show its impact. Streets will be improved through the removal of signs, new lighting and street furniture (see Figure 8.73). Work has also been initiated into the feasibility of eliminating overhead wires and supporting poles in the centre. Alstom have for two years been testing their Aliss system (see Figure 8.75) which provides current in sections, below the tram as it passes along a road. A full-scale test will, if successful, eliminate the overhead wires serving trams, at least in the historic areas.

Integration with other systems   Any light rail system, to be profitable, has to attract the maximum number of passengers on to it and it is in suburban areas that the problem can lie, if densities are low and car ownership high by placing an emphasis on access to stops by car and the need to provide for parking. So far people prefer light rail to bus, because it is more reliable, faster and more comfortable. The percentage of passengers who switch from driving to taking the tram can vary from 20 per cent upwards and cheap parking space is difficult to integrate successfully into the environment. In France, where land is cheap and plentiful, there seems less inhibition in providing for park-and-ride, at strategic points along a light rail route. Planners however, justifiably regard park-and-ride as generating unwanted traffic, causing visual blight and disliked by people living nearby and unpleasant to cross for those walking to a stop. Yet, if it is not provided, then parking will occur close to stops in neighbouring residential streets unless controlled. The priority around most suburban stops should be to provide for good access on foot, by cycle, bus and for kiss-and-ride. In some cases, as has occurred in Portland (see Figure 2.10) multi-storeyed parking is an alternative.

Strasbourg has built a new park-and-ride station, designed by the architect Zaha Hadid, for 750 cars, which forms a spectacular gateway to the city for car drivers (see p. 147) as well as aiming to provide a piece of three-dimensional sculpture. Over 2,000 park-and-ride spaces will be provided in Strasbourg at

Insulating joint   Transmitter   1 power collector

PCC

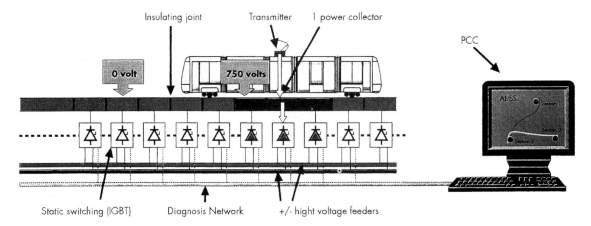

0 volt

750 volts

ALISS

Static switching (IGBT)   Diagnosis Network   +/- hight voltage feeders

8.75
Alstom's experimental Aliss ground-power collection system for light rail vehicles. This is intended to eliminate overhead wires in sensitive historic areas. The drawing shows how switching modules below the track supply voltage once a signal has been detected.

8.76
Shows this subsurface duct with modules which, when powered, provide current to the vehicle above. Courtesy: Alstom Transport SA.

various points around the periphery of the city, removed from the centre. Montpellier with a population of 420,000 people in its region has a high car ownership of 41 cars for every 100 inhabitants and provides parking for a total of 2,000 cars outside, along its light rail line. Feeder buses run to 4 of its 28 stations, with cycle parking at all stations and new cycle lanes provided alongside some of the lines. The residential density along its first line is high, with 75,000 people living within a five-minute walk of stops. Two new stops will be open when development

8.77

Strasbourg, France. Park and ride terminus at Hoenheim-Nord on the Line B tramway for the Compagnie des Transports Strasbourgeois. Aerial view looking along approach tramway with terminus on left together with bus station. The two car parks for a total of 800 cars are designed to provide a sculptural element at the scale of the landscape. Each parking space has a vertical light post of varying heights, depending on the site gradient. Photo: Roger Rothan Air Diesol.

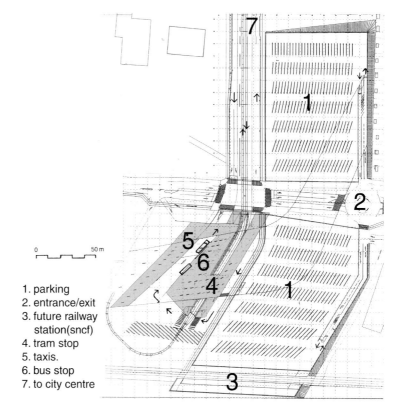

8.78

Strasbourg. Layout plan showing car park circulation, tram and bus station with waiting space, cycle storage and a shop. The idea is to create an 'energetic and attractive space, through three-dimensional graphics of light and openings'. Structural engineer: Luigi Martino. Architect: Zaha Hadid.

0   50 m

1. parking
2. entrance/exit
3. future railway station(sncf)
4. tram stop
5. taxis.
6. bus stop
7. to city centre

8.79
View of Strasbourg tram terminus showing the remarkable cantilevers obtained. Tram stops are shown on left. Engineer: Luigi Martino. Architect: Zaha Hadid. Photo: Helene Binet.

adjacent is complete and relatively easy to provide compared with the complexity of doing this with an elevated or underground system.

Croydon, in south London, in completing its 28 km long system, in contrast with the French examples discussed, has deliberately provided for no park-and-ride at any station. The line connects with two main line stations and a tube station. No parking has been eliminated in the centre and no visible environmental improvement or reduction of traffic in the centre has occurred as a result.

Providing for easy, cross-platform interchange between light rail and bus is important. The example of Montpellier's Corum station shows how small buses circulate within the core area stopping 'on demand' and picking up passengers, unload under a glazed roof also covering the light rail platform. Provision for secure, ideally covered, cycle parking at every light rail stop is also essential at

8.80
Montpellier, France. Interchange station at Corum situated at the edge of the pedestrianised centre. 'Petit buses' on the right (carrying up to 30 passengers), which have picked up people within the historic area, are shown serving the light-rail stop situated below a high-level glazed roof.

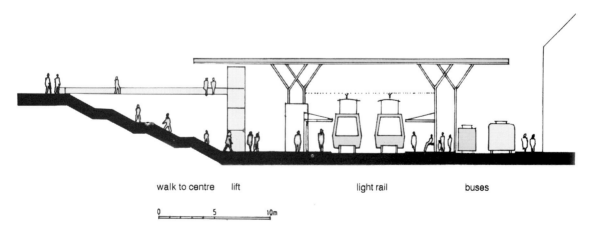

walk to centre   lift   light rail   buses

0   5   10m

8.81
Section, showing stairs, with a lift on the left connecting with the central park and shopping area.

stops within residential areas. Light rail in the larger cities is now being tried as a feeder system, used in conjunction with rail or metro systems. London is planning two feeder systems in the suburbs, to link with tube stations at Greenwich and Shepherd's Bush, with a third line running north–south across the central area from Peckham to Camden to relieve the Northern tube line.

Integration with development   Most light rail systems are being retro-fitted into existing European cities and similarly in North America, while new development areas in Asia are evolving around light rail. At present the planning process in European countries has been less successful in attracting new development around suburban stops than the Portland example (see p. 89) where a reported $1.9 billion worth of development in the first 12 years has occurred along its first line. Developers there, apparently, see a benefit in being close to stops, in spite of high car usage and free parking. In Strasbourg, property values are 10 per cent higher near stops than for other flats in the city centre (Hass-Klau *et al.*, 2000).

In the future, with increasing traffic congestion on roads it is unlikely that in many cities more road space will be built to match demand (in parts of California this has already occurred). It is in these areas that light rail networks could become

8.82
Paris. Light rail running between Bobigny and St Denis showing tracks located between dense public housing with platforms on either side integrated into the development.

an increasingly useful system of public transport. Built at ground level, possibly using the new, lighter designs of vehicle (see p. 136) although slower (average 20 kph; 12 mph), they are a fraction of the cost of conventional metro (average 30 kph; 20 mph). Although most of the systems being built actually take over road space they are still popular with the general public, even car drivers. Achieving this, as has been done in France, is a political issue where, once a mayor supports light rail, it happens – and fast, during his term of office. Above all, as in the examples discussed above, it is done well.

Integrated transport-only connect

Public transport, if it is to compete successfully with the private car, has to provide a comparable service. Cars carry their occupants from door to door, in comfort, and comparative safety, at a perceived low cost, albeit with little regard to the community, yet in the UK average travel distance is less than 2 miles (3.2 km). For public transport to compete it has to be affordable, safe, comfortable, as well as reliable. The system has to be flexible enough to deal with trips that are not necessarily centrally oriented, as well as provide services in reasonable travel times. In future cities new areas, developed at higher densities will allow for public transport to be economic to run. These will be areas where bus or light rail routes are planned from the start, within an environment which will encourage walking and cycling with easy and short access to stops.

Public transport in order to be better used has to be accessible. Ticketing systems have to be compatible with all the systems. Already countries are experimenting with 'smart cards' under a European Commission funding experiment called Concert, which will use them for parking fees as well as bus and rail fares. Cards now used in Hong Kong have built-in memories which will differentiate between charges for different times of day, as well as inform the operators how services are being used (Transport 2000). Travel cards in Germany can allow unlimited travel for a whole year in 56 cities. In Switzerland a 'General pass' gives unlimited travel for the year throughout the country. London's Travelcards increased ridership by 16 per cent when introduced and are used by around 240,000 passengers a day.

Integration between different systems has to be easy and moving towards what airport operators like to call 'seamless travel'. New on-board 'intelligent' technology using global positioning satellite systems now identifies the position at a central control room of every vehicle in a fleet, and informs drivers if they run late. It will ensure that bus services connect with rail or light rail stations, enabling passengers to join services with the minimum waiting time. Buses, for example,

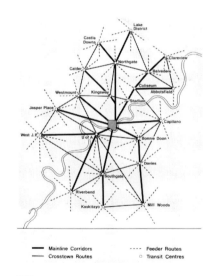

■■■ Mainline Corridors	---- Feeder Routes
── Crosstown Routes	○ Transit Centres

8.83
Edmonton, Alberta. Plan showing bus routes serving areas outside the city centre where 'timed transfer' takes place at interchanges for 80 per cent of the workforce whose jobs are located outside the centre. Courtesy: Edmonton Transit.

8.84
Duivendrecht Station, Holland. An interchange station serving two rail lines – Schiphol Airport to Amsterdam and Amsterdam to Utrecht. Ground-level view showing bus station and kiss-and-ride lay-by at low level with lockers for cyclists.

8.85
Concourse at first floor with clear signs to indicate the interchange levels. The separate lift, shown beyond the escalator on the right, leads down to buses below.

run 'timed transfer services' on seven routes in Portland, Oregon. In Edmonton, Alberta (see Figure 8.83) where car ownership is low, only 20 per cent of commuter trips are to downtown. This allows passengers bound for cross-city trips to change buses at specially designed interchange stations with the minimum of waiting involved. However, this is only possible if buses can run on roads free from congestion from other vehicles.

The need to interchange, however, is one of the factors which travellers like least about public transport. In cities of 500,000 people over 50 per cent of passengers need to interchange. In London 46 per cent of passengers on the Underground make one interchange per trip, with 7 per cent making two. Walking, too, is an important part of every trip, either interchanging or not. Every trip made, either to reach a bus stop, to interchange or finally to reach a required destination, is on foot. The 'perceived' quality of public transport as a result depends on there being close attention to 'detail'. People on their own two feet are acutely aware of their walking environment, more acutely aware of safety, than those who are encapsulated in a private car.

With segregated rail systems, elevated or underground, all new systems will in many countries now provide for lift access, making them accessible not only for the old or physically impaired (Richards, 1990) but also for use by mums with children, pushing buggies. The new Dutch rail stations, such as that shown at Duivendrecht (Edwards, 1997) show consistent attention to these detailed aspects and achieve a high quality of design due to the excellence of their architects working for one enlightened firm called Railconsult. Only lacking in some of these stations is any attempt to relate new planned development around the stations which frequently sit in a wasteland. Surface-level systems of transport have the advantage of being easily accessible. The bus interchange stations in Curitiba, Brazil, for example (see Figure 8.87) show how interchange is achieved at one level, within the ticketed area, from a whole range of local buses feeding on to express buses. This means that adequate space is provided at the planning stage, much easier to achieve outside the central area than within. In France good examples of inter-

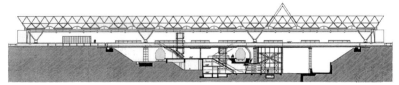

8.86
Section showing access to all platforms by escalators and lifts which serve all three levels. Courtesy: Peter Kilsdonk. Architect: Holland Railconsult.

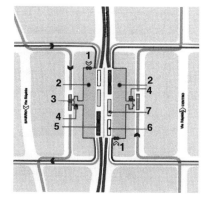

8.87
Curitiba, Brazil. Plan of typical interchange station. Allows for unlimited interchange between services within the ticketed area: (1) station entrances; (2) interchange area; (3) direct line; (4) tubular station; (5) express service; (6) interbarrios service; (7) food shop. Courtesy: URBS.

change between bus and tram are shown at Pirmil station at Nantes (see Figure 8.88), and the Corum station in Montpellier (see p. 149). These examples show how weather-protected interchange is possible with simple, elegant roofs covering both systems. Within city centres, widened pavement space should be provided at bus stops along the kerb edge, particularly where interchanging might take place between different routes. In practice this is rarely done.

Interchange stations will, in the future, need to be planned as focal points in the community, rather than becoming simply park-and-ride points. In many cases they could become places to shop, for small community facilities or offices. Parking takes up valuable land close to station platforms, which would be better either placed underground, in multi-storeyed parking (see p. 60), both costly alternatives or simply not provided. This means that parking controls have then to be extended around the stations into the residential areas, to avoid 'rail-heading'. In the new Skyway extension in Vancouver running through existing residential areas space, the stations will provide only for drop-down for buses of kiss-and-ride with parking for cycles.

By achieving this degree of integration between systems and development public transport could become as easily used, for many trips, as the private car. Such integration requires political commitment with a continuous rolling programme of investment, as well as a system run by dedicated people. Only this will really attract people to use it in future cities.

8.88
Nantes, France. Example of typical bus/light-rail station in the suburbs which provides for cross-platform interchange under a single, simple designed high-level roof.

Conclusions

The frequent reference to the private car in these pages has been a reminder of the present situation. Cars are being bought by more and more people, becoming marginally less polluting, yet being used by drivers, within cities, on ever more congested road space. These are drivers who put up with the fatigue of driving, finding parking and the expense of running their vehicles yet still prefer this as a way of getting to work. For many people the choice of alternative transport is often poor; for others, who have a choice, many still enjoy driving.

At the receiving end is a public, particularly those on foot, having to put up with the rise of traffic, of which a high proportion are cars, with the resulting levels of pollution, danger and noise which they bring as well as with the frustration for others of travelling on buses trapped by other vehicles. With the number of cars predicted in the UK to double in the next 20 years it must surely be concluded by now that with a higher quality of life expected, and with more people moving back into cities, a reduction in car traffic must be part of that process.

In many smaller cities with their centres freed of cars and with excellent public

8.89
Strasbourg. An example of the exceptionally high quality of detailed finish to the pedestrian routes radiating from the centre closely integrated with the tram routes and their stops.

transport serving them, this is happening. But in the larger cities it is not – the politics are more problematic, as well as the scale of what has to be done and the cost of doing it. These are cities where traffic is regarded by many as an inevitable fact of life, which cannot be changed or reduced – 'the lifeblood of the city', which need not be the case.

To summarise the key measures which have been discussed and which have to be made, if there is to be any improvement in the long term:

- High-tech means of maximising road space, with automated freeways, lane metering or area wide traffic control, are unlikely to solve long-term traffic problems, neither is increased road building.
- Road pricing and parking charges are both practical ways of making the motorist pay towards the true cost of driving within cities, as well as help fund good public transport.
- Within city centres, conventional ownership of private cars may in the long term be largely replaced by car clubs, with smart cars reducing car ownership in cities.
- Planning and design of new parts of cities and their buildings must consider access by public transport.
- Planning housing to a higher density is important, in transport terms, to help reduce travel distances. Clustering of mixed development around transport stops should be part of this.
- Walking is an essential part of any transport system and all trips start and finish on foot. The quality of the environment for pedestrians should be given the highest priority.
- Cycling is an important mode of transport and safe conditions must be provided, such as slower roads and cycle lanes.
- Public transport systems for short distance travel must be provided, such as hail to stop buses in residential areas, for local trips.
- Surface-level transport networks of systems, such as light rail, or express bus routes, will benefit more people, at less cost, if provided along many corridors, rather than single high-capacity metros built along one corridor.
- All public transport systems must be to a standard sufficiently comfortable, convenient and safe to get people out of their cars.

The end result of these combined strategies could help make cities safer, cleaner and more enjoyable places in which to live and work. Many people want to move back into them and the means to improve the quality of life there is possible. Improving transport has to be part of the solution to achieve any change. Only the political will is needed to make this happen.

COMPARATIVE PLANS OF TRANSPORT SYSTEMS	COMPARATIVE SECTIONS TWO-WAY OPERATION	TURNING RADII	ECONOMIC DISTANCE BETWEEN STOPS	PASSENGER OR VEHICLE CAPACITY PER HOUR ONE WAY	AVERAGE SPEED
PEDESTRIANS				10,15,000	4.8 km /hr. 3 mph
BICYCLES				2-5,000	16 km /hr. 10 mph
MOVING PAVEMENT		straight	100-400m.	6,000	2.5 km/hr 1.5 mph
ACCELERATING MOVING PAVEMENT (Accel-liner)		straight & curved	100-400 m.	6,000	7.5 km/hr 4.5 mph.
PRIVATE CAR ON SURFACE STREET				700-900 v.p.hr.	13-24 km / hr. 8-15 mph
MINIBUS		6 m. 20'	400-500 m 500 yd.	120 vph. 3,600	10-15 km/hr 6-30 mphr.
DOUBLE DECK BUS ON CITY STREET		21m 70"	3-400 m. 500 yd.	120 vph. 7,200	13-24 km / hr. 8-15 mph.
EXPRESS BUS ON SEPARATE LANE		20m.	1610 m.	1,450 vphr.	88.5 km/hr.
GUIDED BUS ON SEPARATE LANES		20 m. 70'		120 vph. 10,000	100 km /hr. 62 mph.

Scale at top:
COMPARATIVE PLANS OF TRANSPORT SYSTEMS — metres 10 0 20 40; feet 0 10 50 100
COMPARATIVE SECTIONS TWO-WAY OPERATION — metres 0 5 10; feet 0 5 10 20 30

8.90

Tables showing the systems discussed, each drawn to the same scale (shown at the top). The plans of each (on the left) are shown at one scale. The cross sections at a larger scale are on the right. The four columns on the right show the physical characteristics of each system.

COMPARATIVE PLANS OF TRANSPORT SYSTEMS	COMPARATIVE SECTIONS TWO-WAY OPERATION	TURNING RADII	ECONOMIC DISTANCE BETWEEN STOPS	PASSENGER OR VEHICLE CAPACITY PER HOUR ONE WAY	AVERAGE SPEED
MINIRAIL (Intamin)		24 m 80'	600 m ·5 mile	4-5,000	50 km/hr 30 mph.
ARTICULATED THREE-CAR TRAM		15-30 m 50-100'	400-800 m 1200 '	10-20,000	32- 50 km/hr 20-30 mph.
GUIDED LIGHT TRANSIT (Bombardier)		12 m. 40'	4-500 m 1200'	10,000	32-50 km /hr 20-30 mph.
VAL SYSTEM (Matra)		40 m 120'	1-2 km. 1·7 mile	10-30,000	35 km /hr 21 mph
SHUTTLE TRANSIT (Otis)		18-90 m 60-300'	500 m ·5 mile	3-8,000	40 km/hr 25mph.
SKYTRAIN		35 m 120'	1-2 km. 1·7 mile	7,500	47 km /hr. 29 mph.
MONORAIL (Alweg· Hitachi)		46 m. 150'	1-2 km. 1 mile	10-30,000	40 km/hr. 25 mph.
GUIDEWAY TRANSIT Adtranz)		22 m 72 '	1-2 km · 7 mile	8,000	30 km / hr 20mph
UNDERGROUND METRO		101m. 330'	1-3 km. ·5-2 mile	20-40.00	32-50 km/hr. 20-30 mph

metres 10   0   20   40
feet   0 10   50   100

metres 0   5   10
feet   0 5 10 20   30

Selected bibliography

Beatley, T. (2000) *Green Urbanism: Learning from European Cities*, Washington DC: Island Press.

Cervero, R. (1938) *The Transit Metropolis: A Global Enquiry*, Washington DC: Island Press.

Edwards, B. (1997) *The Modern Station*, London: E&FN Spon–Chapman & Hall.

European Community (1999) 'Cycling: the way ahead for towns and cities', *DGXI.Boulevard du Triomphe*, 174 B-1160.Brussels.

Franklin, J. (1999) 'Two decades of the Redway', *Milton Keynes. Traffic Engineering & Control*, London.

Hass-Klau, C., Crampton, G. *et al.* (2000) *Bus or Light Rail: Making the Right Choice*, Brighton: Environmental & Transport Planning.

HUD (Department of Housing and Urban Development) (1968) *Future Urban Transportation Systems*, Stanford CA: Stanford Research Institute.

Mitchell, W.J. (2000) *E-Topia: Urban Life, Jim – But Not as We Know It*, Boston: MIT Press.

Newman, P. and Kenworthy, J. (1999) *Sustainability and Cities*, Washington DC: Island Press.

Howard, J. (2000) 'Driving in my telematic car', *Observer* 1 October.

Pharoah, T. and Apel, D. (1995) *Concepts in European Cities*, Aldershot: Ashgate.

Plowden, S. (1980) *Taming Traffic*, London: André Deutsch.

Richards, B. (1966) *New Movement in Cities*, London and New York: Studio Vista/Reinhold.

Richards, B. (1976) *Moving in Cities*, London: Studio Vista.

Richards, B. (1990) *Transport in Cities*, London: ADT Press.

Shaheen, C., Sperling, D. and Wagner, C. (1999) 'Carsharing and Partnership Management', *Transportation Research Record 1666 TRB*, National Research Council, Washington DC, 118–24.

Sorkin, M. (1992) *Variations on a Theme Park*, New York: Hill & Wang (Trevor Boddy – Underground & Overhead).

Transport 2000 (1997) *Blueprint for Quality Public Transport*, London: Transport 2000 Trust.

Urban Task Force (1999) *Towards an Urban Renaissance*, London: E & FN Spon.

Warren, R. (1998) *The Urban Oasis*, New York: McGraw-Hill.

Index

Page numbers appearing in **bold** refer to illustrations.